"Baars was the hit of the Fortune Magazine summit."

Verne Harnish, bestselling author of *Scaling Up*, Founder Entrepreneurs' Organization (EO)

"A fresh, exciting and insightful perspective on what motivates and drives us."

""This book offers ideas outside the range of thinking of most success books. One of the most compelling and fascinating arguments the author makes is that our happiness today does not come from today, rather it depends upon how we see tomorrow. I look forward to reading it again in order to glean every last juicy morsel of insight and wisdom from it.." —Harvey Deutschendorf, author of *The Other Kind of Smart: Simple Ways to Boost Your Emotional Intelligence for Greater Personal Effectiveness and Success*, writes regularly for FAST COMPANY magazine and HR PROFESSIONALS magazine

"In his new book, Rabbi Baars has reconfigured the concept of winning. On each page you can hear him speaking directly to you with wisdom and encouragement that could change your life." —Rebecca Gabriel, author of *Woman's Journey – A Life in Paintings*

Praise for "Think Like A Winner" Program & Workshop

"It is worth every second of your time and every penny of the cost." —Javier Goldin, Managing Partner, Goldin Group LLC

"If you want to improve the way you think and feel about life this workshop is for you!" —Jamey Charapp
"The content resonated so deeply within me." —Claire Dwoskin

"It is not about what happens to you. It is about how you think about what happens to you that changes everything!" —C Gilman

D1509745

Also by Stephen Baars

BOOKS

The Worst Marriage Advice in the World

Bliss: The Marriage AND Parenting Book

SEMINARS & VIDEOS

Bliss

How to Think Like a Winner

Elevator Parenting (a video series)

The Essential Hero

Are You a Penguin—Inspirational Life Lessons

Be the Reason for Being

The Bully Cure

3 Steps to Great Self-Confidence

Superman has NOTHING on you!

WIN.

WIN.

Change Your Thinking, Change Your Destiny

Rabbi Stephen Baars

Wellstone Press

ISBN: 978-1-930835-21-4
Library of Congress Number
2018930842

10 9 8 7 6 5 4 3 2 1

WELLSTONE PRESS
wellstonepress.com

Contents

Introduction

On May 11, 1997, for the first time ever a machine beat a world chess champion.

It was Garry Kasparov and he lost to IBM's Deep Blue.

As one might expect, humanity fought back.

Revenge came eight years later in a variant of chess called "freestyle." Freestyle is chess with more collaboration.

In this tournament, grandmasters were pitched against all kinds of other players, even with state-of-the-art Deep Blue level computers.

But the shock came when two *amateur* American players won out with nothing more than regular off-the-shelf computers. (Source: nybooks.com 2010)

Kasparov, who is regarded by many as the greatest chess player of all time, explained the deep significance of this moment: The best minds in the world, even if matched with the best computers in the world, are no match against anyone with a superior technique.

Kasparov's point is this: You don't have to be a genius,

chess or otherwise. You don't need the best tools, computers or otherwise. You just need the right ideas.

Whether that is George Washington taking on the superpower of his time, the British in 1776, or, exactly 200 years later, Steve Jobs taking on the titans of the computing industry in 1976, the little guy has the upper hand if he, or she, has the right ideas.

Winners don't have more stamina. They just have better ideas. They don't have higher IQs. They just have great strategy. They don't have phenomenal talent. They just have clever technique.

Bill Gates noted that even though Microsoft had more money and much of the same technology as Steve Jobs and Apple, Jobs was nevertheless able to become the leader in the tech world because he had the right ideas.

Great ideas are what will transform the same effort you are now exerting into phenomenal results, and that freestyle chess match proves the point—the amateurs that won did not do so through greater effort, skill, or even intelligence. And although they were outflanked on all of these, they beat the best by doing what humans do best: Thinking.

There is a vast ocean of excellent books, brilliantly detailing what the great winners did to succeed. **And if you simply follow and do what they did, you will never be a winner**—at least not on their level.

You have to think like they think, because it's that very thinking that made them do what they did.

If you want to win, then you too have to think like a winner. This is the absolute and only key to success. You have to think in ways that make you win.

What this book will do for you is change your thinking— **just by reading it.**

When you change your thinking you will change your life.

Change your thinking, change your life. Change your destiny.

It's that easy. And for it to work it has to be easy. Because, if it isn't easy, it won't work!

Part 1

CHAPTER 1

Winning Made Easy

Fifteen or so grizzled, cynical, and more than a few desperate men sit in a circle in a halfway house in a part of Los Angeles that you wouldn't normally go to unless you were lost: *In life that is.*

I'm the sixteenth, and the odd one out. The contrast is surreal. I'm there because I am supposed to impart wisdom.

Most of those fifteen are at least twice my age and, apart from me, significant abusers of alcohol and illegal substances.

Looking back at that moment, it is a mystery to me as to why they listened to anything I had to say. The unofficial qualification for speaking to any group of abusers is very simple: You have to be, or have been, a member of the club.

I was not.

With self-abuse there is no faking it. And I wouldn't know where to begin even if I'd wanted to try. Up until that moment my only experience with alcoholics was an old Jimmy Stewart movie. I clearly did not have the creds to be in that room.

But the organizing social worker needed a guest speaker, and they couldn't come up with anyone better than me, the new rabbi in town.

I was so green I had no appreciation of what a bad idea this was. Yet there I was, on the spot, with all eyes on me and all waiting for me to deliver inspiration.

When I got home I called a surprised social worker, not sure if the surprise was because I was still alive or because the group wanted me back.

But on that day, as the men went around the room telling their indelibly troubled stories, my anxiety kept notching up, one painful tale at a time.

This was show-and-tell, but it wasn't finger painting. This was put your misery on the table and it had better be bad. My mind scrambled to at least match the bitterness these souls had endured.

I played my own tales of woe in my head—after all, we all have painful moments. But in comparison, my tragedies seemed pathetic.

Ever since then, one man in particular has remained highlighted in my brain. In terms of age, he could easily have been my grandfather. He'd suffered from alcoholism and had been in and out of prison most of his adult life. To me his story was one of excruciating pain, yet to him, it was one of joy because it ended with the accomplishment of which he was proudest: For the first time in his entire life he experienced the thrill of legitimately earning a paycheck!

Others described blatant abuse, both self-inflicted and not.

As is the custom of AA meetings, and this was no exception, they talked about their rock bottom—the moment for a person when there is no more down to go, and the only option is up.

Strange, isn't it? We are willing to destroy our lives until we each reach a point where we know we can't destroy it anymore.

Little did I realize that leading this group would result in a similar turning point for me—as I listened and learned from those men a tremendous misconception started to unravel.

I had previously thought that rock bottom is the point when a person becomes willing to take on the pain, to do that which they were previously unable.

But that is clearly not true. I have seen too many people reach that point, pause, and then keep on going down.

Rock bottom is not the point at which a person is willing to be tough. These people did not suddenly decide to try and put their lives together—the pain in their faces and in their stories clearly demonstrated they were always trying to do that.

An alcoholic has not given up on life. Every day he's trying to put his life back together, but he can't. He can't because he thinks he's not tough enough.

Rock bottom is actually the point when you give up trying to be tough.

Allow me to show you how this idea might exhibit itself in your own life, and how changing your thinking will open up all kinds of new opportunities.

Think of the challenges that you are struggling with right now. Let us use a common one, dieting, as an illustration of many others.

Your anguish about dieting is precisely because you have not given up. You are working hard at it, but your efforts just are not giving you the results you want.

And they won't work until you give up thinking you need to be tougher to conquer the diet challenge. This simple insight will change everything you are struggling with. You don't need to be more disciplined to succeed—you simply need to make your goals easier.

Making your goals easier is not the same as finding easier goals, a nuance that may sound small, but is worlds apart.

It's the difference between the Wright brothers trying to conquer flight by learning from birds (making a great goal easier), or just making a bigger hot air balloon (an easy goal).

It's the difference between Edison forming a lab of scientists to invent a light bulb (making a great goal easier) or simply making a really big candle (an easy goal).

It's the difference between Henry Ford automating car production to build an affordable car (making a great goal easier), or just breeding faster horses (easy goal).

No success in life will come from simply choosing easy goals. Instead, it will come from making your tough goals easy.

Not only is making tough goals easy the way to succeed—it is the only way anyone succeeds!

Successful people are not tougher. They may appear that way, but it's an illusion. Instead they have found a way to make their tough goals achievable for who they are, and everyone else has not. They appear tough because they are doing things that we find hard—but that they, actually, find easy.

I am sure you do things that your friends wish they could do, and they do things that you wish you could. Everyone thinks everyone else is tough, but the truth is that no one is! Everyone is simply doing that which they find easy.

An elephant is not tough! Yes, it can uproot a tree, but for an elephant yanking a tree from the ground is a piece of cake.

A cheetah is not strong. Yes, it can run seventy-five miles an hour, but that's how it is made—both of these animals are only doing what they find easy.

For a cheetah to uproot a tree, or an elephant to run as fast as a cheetah, would be tough. But they both do what they find easy, and because of this they both end up successful. And so will you!

Whoever knows how to make the tough easy, will find immense success; whoever has immense success has figured out how to make their goal easy.

Let's take this deeper.

It's not just that you don't need to be tougher. You can't be any more tough than you are now.

A horse has a top speed of approximately thirty miles an hour. It isn't going to run a hundred miles an hour if you put a bigger carrot in front of it, or whip it harder. It's built for thirty, and it can't do any more than that. Similarly, you and I are as tough as we are ever going to be.

Western thinking has got us believing that to succeed we need to find some new reservoir of strength—the problem is it doesn't exist. You can't find or dig a new reservoir that really isn't there.

What you can do is what all successful people do: Use what you have to get everything you want.

Finding a way to make your goals easy is the secret.

But easy doesn't mean lower, or even realistic.

This is important.

When people tell you to choose realistic goals, what they

really mean is to lower your goals. But this philosophy is fundamentally flawed, because when a person lowers their aspirations for something more "realistic," what they have also done is made the goal less inspiring. And, of course, less motivating.

Paradoxically the more "realistic," or lower, or so-called "attainable," a goal is, the more unattainable it really becomes. A lower goal is actually less appealing, and equally, less motivating.

Imagine if Steve Jobs set out to make a more advanced calculator, or if Edison dreamed of brighter candles, where would the world be?

I can tell you, we'd be no better off. I also doubt either of those people could be motivated to achieve either of those goals.

The reason we have lofty goals is because that's what gets our juices going. You might as well tell someone to give up now if you are trying to convince them to choose "realistic" goals. Instead, we need to match those lofty goals with a method that makes it easy.

I have been teaching this idea for many years, all over the world, and an amazing thing happens when a student gets it and the imaginary light bulb in their head goes off (I hope this is what is happening to you now). It's a magical moment when they realize how transformative this idea is in everything they are striving for.

Try this: Place every goal you have ever given up on into a bucket. Now notice the one consistent theme that is true for all of those ambitions. They all are in that bucket for the same reason—because you thought you were not tough enough to succeed.

Now, pick up any one of those goals and ask a different question. "If it were easy to achieve, would I still want it?"

In this book I am going to show you how to make your goals easy and keep you motivated.

Take a look at this list of common issues:

Angry	Honest
Impatient	Unorganized
Alcohol	Disciplined
Calm	Lazy
Loving	Indecisive
Food	Loyal
Trusting	Arrogant
Kind	Enthusiastic
Studious	Drugs
Fearful	Friendly
Self-Confident	Worried

If you are struggling with any one of those issues, cross it off the list. (Perhaps your issue is not on the list—that's fine.) Now look at the remaining issues and realize how many great things you have going for you—well done! These are the things you have conquered.

Now, were you able to conquer them because you are tough? Undoubtedly no.

These issues are simply not a challenge for you. For you they are easy.

However, your issues, the ones not on the list or that you crossed off, for someone who doesn't have them as a given, they're easy too.

Here is the incredible thing: When you think about your issues, the ones you struggle with, the same way those other people think about them, then they will be easy for you too!

Winners are not people built with super human strength. Rather, they are people just like us, who have figured out how to do this exact thing!

Successful people learned the same thing those recovering alcoholics learned—that we won't achieve anything important in life if we believe we have to be tough.

No one has that much strength.

Sir Richard Branson, founder of the Virgin Group, is one of the richest men alive with a net worth of approximately $5.1 billion (*Forbes*). He is also extremely dyslexic. He didn't get to where he is by being frustrated. Amongst his disabilities is that he can't tell the difference between gross and net profit. To be honest with you, I would not have believed that if I had not heard him say it.

He owns approximately four hundred different companies, ranging from soft drinks to airlines, wedding dresses to cell phones. How can you build such an empire and not know the difference between gross and net?

Simple. He figured out how to make what he wanted easy.

"A business has to be involving, it has to be fun, and it has to exercise your creative instincts."
—Sir Richard Branson

This book will explain how highly successful people actually achieve their goals, often using their own words as examples of their mentality. It will dispel the myths of why most people never attain their dreams.

Winners don't have more stamina, or built-in genius, they have just learned how to think in ways that get them the results they want.

And they never lower their goals. Never!

Here is another incredible idea: Highly successful people weren't born thinking that way. They learned how.

You can learn to think that way too.

Let me explain how it all came together for me.

Back in L.A., working with those people in the halfway house had been overwhelming and humbling. Those men had overcome something most never do. The scale of their accomplishments made anything I had done seem no more difficult than breathing in and breathing out.

A person who has conquered drugs or alcohol has overcome an obstacle that is so vast that an equal distance traveled in our own lives would afford us a life we can only dream of. If you think of how low an alcoholic gets, but then turns it around and pulls his life together, it's a colossal and amazing journey.

How then did these people overcome such an obstacle when previously a single bottle of beer would have stopped them in their tracks?

This is so important I want to repeat it. For alcoholics, the thought of being sober is harder than any goal most people have probably ever imagined.

And so imagine if the rest of humanity learned from them.

As I continued to work with that group, I tried to impart a consistent theme. "You, the people sitting in this room, are not the problem. You are the ones who decided to go for it. It's the rest of society, it is they who have given up."

And while that message resonated with those souls, it is that very message that has frustrated me to this day. The people in that program were not the problem—it is the people not in it who are.

If the rest of humanity tried to improve the quality of their lives to the same degree as a recovering alcoholic, then so many of the problems plaguing us all would be solved.

Now realize what we have just concluded.

It could not possibly be that those people in the halfway house, who previously succumbed to the smallest of challenges, had become super tough. They didn't grit their teeth and bite down on the bullet of self-sacrifice to pull their lives together.

There had to be something else going on to explain how they achieved so much.

I have nothing but admiration for people who overcome these kinds of obstacles. But they didn't do it by being strong. Yes, they got strength from their accomplishments, but strength wasn't the secret ingredient that got them on the right path.

My mission is to describe that secret ingredient so that you can use it too.

In the twenty-five years since those sessions I have had the unique honor of counseling thousands of people on a multitude of issues. I am most grateful for the people I was able to help. But I am equally frustrated by the ones I could not help. Why couldn't these people find the advice they needed? Are some people destined for misery and failure?

I simply could not countenance such a concept.

There had to be a formula for all human beings to get out of the messes in which we are so good at getting ourselves into.

You probably think me naïve to even suggest such a concept, but no one thinks Albert Einstein juvenile for seeking a universal truth.

Einstein, convinced there must be a theory behind the seemingly random and disparate laws of physics known at the time, was driven by a single thought: To find the one formula that would explain the entire physical universe—the Unified Field Theory.

I too became driven, thinking there must be a single underlying principle that could help everyone win no matter what the issue or who the person.

Why couldn't we bottle what a recovering alcoholic is now drinking and give it to everyone else to overcome the challenges they are facing?

It took a very long time, but I found what I was seeking in ancient Jewish teachings thousands of years old. Clearly I was not the first to ponder this question. Far greater people had walked that path.

After successfully applying what I found to marriage and parenting, I became intrigued and decided to apply these concepts to business, which is how this book and the "Think Like a Winner" seminar series were conceived.

People think life is meant to be hard. And, if they can't hack it, then they believe the good life is not meant for them. There is no end to how mediocre or decrepit you will let your life become when you think you are not tough enough to make it.

An alcoholic can attest to that.

But the reality is quite the opposite, the really good life is easy—and it's meant to be easy. And when life is easy, life is good.

Sports, business, food, friendships and family, are only truly enjoyed by those who have figured out how to make them easy. These are the winners.

This is not a paradox.

People who work "hard" at anything, and therefore succeed, are the ones who find it easy. They find it easy because they love doing it. For everyone else it seems hard because they just don't enjoy it.

"I never did a day's work in my life. It was all fun."
—Thomas A. Edison

Thus, telling someone to work harder is completely counter-productive. Not only won't they work harder, but most likely all they will do is fake it, and as they fake it they will grow more resentful and achieve less.

Doesn't our experience with alcoholics prove this? When everyone around them tells them to pull themselves together and overcome their abuse, what happens?

They fake it until their lives fall apart.

If you are someone who struggles with exercise, or food, or work, and were charged with running a marathon or following a strict diet, or tripling your work output, would you not find such a goal overwhelming? Then how did an alcoholic come to have the power over something so much more debilitating and controlling?

As we have been explaining, their success is not due to a sudden ability to be strong. Similarly, we aren't going to overcome our frustrations by drinking some super potion that will transform us into a man or woman of steel. Rather, they didn't get tough, they figured out how to make it easy.

They gave up thinking that the only way to succeed is to be tough, and instead took the capabilities they already had and used them to achieve the goal they really wanted.

As long as you think you need what you don't have, you will never get what you really want.

If a life-long substance abuser can overcome previously insurmountable obstacles, shouldn't we be able to do the same with our goals?

Not by being tough, but by figuring out how to make it easy.

If you want someone to work harder, the secret is showing them how to enjoy it more so they will want to work harder.

Isn't this obvious? Do we have to tell anyone to eat more ice cream, or take more vacations, or play more golf, or enjoy family and friends more often?

When human beings enjoy something, they work really hard at it.

Those friends of mine in the halfway house weren't there because they were willing to do what was tough; they were there because they learned to enjoy trying to be sober and clean.

That doesn't mean you should do what is easy. It means that when you know what you really want, then your goal is to figure out how to make it easy.

If you don't love it, then you haven't found your way to easy.

Paul Akers is an exceptionally talented and highly successful businessman, who I am privileged to call one of my mentors. He explains in his very helpful book, *Lean Health*, how he conquered the perennial challenge of eating right.

I should point out that Paul is far from anyone's definition of a slacker. He built and continues to run a multi-million dollar business, travels the world teaching his unique business philosophy, and keeps an exhausting schedule. Yet he finds time for friends, family, working out, and writing books (he just finished his second).

But he wasn't tough enough to conquer food.

How could this be?

Because his long list of accomplishments had nothing to do with his degree of strength, it had to do with his love of those things.

What he loved, he did, and did well.

What he eventually discovered in food is exactly what I am pointing out. He couldn't discipline himself to do what he knew he should. He had tried that many times over, all with the same poor results. Eventually, he tapped into the part of himself that liked the things he knew he needed to eat—now he doesn't need to think about eating properly, he naturally wants to.

Pushing yourself to do what is hard is like trying to bring a mountain to you. Doing what you like is you paying a visit to the mountain.

You probably know what it is you need to do to be more successful. You also know that you don't do it because it's too painful. It isn't enjoyable, so it isn't easy.

This book will give you the tools and concepts to make it easy.

It's not about pushing yourself even though it is hard, it's about figuring out how to make it easy and fun. And you will figure it out, as long as you don't give up.

When it's fun you aren't pushing yourself, the goal itself is pulling you along. To everyone else it looks like you are tough and disciplined, but to you, the person doing it, it feels natural and easy.

If you have ever met anyone who loves jogging, they will tell you that if they miss a day they feel terrible. They aren't pushing themselves to run, rather, their love of the sport is pulling them to get up at the crack of dawn and run twenty miles. However, you can be certain, that they too have areas in their lives they struggle with. And they probably wonder, "If I can be tough enough to run a marathon, why can't I control my anger?" Or drinking habits. Or any other issue. The reason should now be obvious.

The reason we think highly successful people are tough is because we try to put ourselves in their shoes and imagine achieving what they have achieved. And therefore we conclude that the only way for us to win like them is to be tough.

I know people who love to exercise—they do it whenever they can—but they aren't tougher than me, they are simply doing what they enjoy just as much as I do what I enjoy. And, this is where it is relevant to you, my dear reader, when you figure out how to enjoy the goals you really want, then absolutely any and every goal is available to you.

> *The only limits you have in life are from those things you haven't yet learned to enjoy.*

> *This is my unified field theory of living.*

"If you don't love it, you are going to fail."
—Steve Jobs

CHAPTER 2
The Big Easy

On your way home from work a fire truck speeds by. Then another. In the distance you can see smoke rising in the general direction of your home. Disturbing thoughts enter your mind as you drive up your street.

Fear and trepidation fill your head, and your pulse starts to race.

Too many fire trucks crowd your front lawn and blazing flames pour out of your windows. Without turning off the engine you rush to the front door, only to be tackled by the fire chief who shouts, "Are you crazy! You can't go in there!"

"You don't understand," you reply, pushing him aside. "My three year old is in there!"

What makes you go in?

It's not bravery and it's not guts, it's simply an idea that precludes any ability to consider the terrible odds of survival.

Ideas—in this case "My three year old is in there"—are the secret motivators to success. The idea of your child being trapped in the house, crying for you, choking on smoke, is pure energy.

This is rocket fuel, and it makes you do something even a trained fireman won't do, and more importantly, can't do.

You would be mistaken if you thought it was you. It isn't.

You would also be mistaken if you thought it was the situation. It's not that either.

Rather, it's the thought that transforms you and the situation into the extraordinary.

That specific situation is gratefully rare, but every situation, and in fact life itself, is a situation waiting for its idea. Whoever is fortunate enough to formulate that idea, no matter who they are, no matter what the situation, will achieve something amazing.

Life is a situation waiting for its idea.

One of my children was absolutely convinced that it was impossible to ride a bicycle. The fact that millions of people do it was inadmissible as evidence.

No matter what I said, she wouldn't budge.

That is until one day her younger sibling mastered it. After that, she learned to ride—that very day!

What happened?

This child really believed riding a bicycle was impossible. Really! That is how she really thought.

But seeing her sibling learn to ride changed her thinking. The idea that her younger brother could do something she couldn't was incredibly motivating.

Suddenly, the belief that it was impossible became irrelevant.

Ideas don't make the impossible possible, they make the impossible irrelevant.

In worlds not too dissimilar from our own, people who we

call winners came to think about life in ways that inevitably put them on paths that ensured their place in history.

You can think that way too.

It's not what they did that made them a success. It's what they thought.

It doesn't matter what challenging experiences you have lived through. If you do just a little research you will find someone who has gone through worse, and achieved ten times more.

How did they end up better off?

It's not luck or circumstances. It's not that they were in the right place at the right time. And it is certainly not that they were built from different stuff than you.

It's not what they did that made them winners. It's how they thought that made winning inevitable.

Everyone encounters multiple opportunities to achieve success, but the person with the right ideas and way of thinking will be the one who takes advantage of those opportunities.

How do we have to think to be the person we want to be? It is not as hard as you might imagine.

Let's examine this in the negative.

Tell a cancer patient he only has three months to live, and in all probability that idea alone will cause him such despair he might not even make it to that marker. That's why it's common for doctors to say nothing.

Not a bullet, nor a runaway train, but simply an idea killed him.

If a bad or negative idea can kill a person, then just imagine what a positive idea can do.

I am sure you can come up with ten negative thoughts that could easily turn you into a lethargic mess of blubber. But can you think of ten ideas that would turn you into a multi-billionaire? What about the ideas you would need to drop the weight you want to lose, or to be the incredible mom/dad/ friend you would like to be admired as?

What ideas would you need to transform your company or business? Or yourself?

Do you understand how powerful this is? When you get the idea, then you don't have a choice. It makes incredible success inevitable.

Steve Jobs was infected with an idea that made him shake up the world. He could hardly help himself from not going down in the history books.

But you too have ideas that similarly propel you. A human being doesn't get out of bed in the morning without an idea. That idea might be "work" or "vacation" or "breakfast."

But, without thinking about the day ahead, we just don't move. That is why, when the day's prospects look bleak, it's hard to actually get out of bed.

Your level of activity is a product of your ideas. It might be true that negative thoughts are dragging you down. But just realize what you would be able to do if you could fill your head with positive ones.

That level of activity is easy for you to maintain. In fact, it would be difficult to do less. Just note all the things you did today and imagine not doing them—it's hard to even consider it.

For example, your thinking won't let you skip brushing your teeth in the morning. Therefore, if you thought about exercising or dieting or whatever you wanted to conquer, in the same way as brushing your teeth, then everything would be available to you.

It is thus a colossal mistake to think that achieving more would be more difficult.

It simply wouldn't. That is, if you can think about achieving more in the same way you think about what you are doing now, which you do so effortlessly.

Once you find this new way of thinking, then it will actually be hard to operate at your current level.

Let me explain.

If you are a smoker, the thought of not smoking seems incredibly challenging. The same goes for not drinking alcohol. Or the idea of exercising regularly. Or dieting.

The thought of overcoming an obstacle like an addiction, or starting a good habit, seems Herculean.

But, if you don't smoke or drink, if you do exercise regularly and eat appropriately, then for you to continue along these paths is not hard at all. In fact, it takes no effort whatsoever to continue to not smoke, not drink, or to show up at the gym and have a tofu salad for lunch.

In fact, for the non-smoker to take up smoking would be incredibly difficult.

We all know people who are challenged with what we take for granted, and others who find what we are struggling with a breeze.

If those who are challenged by what is easy for us would think about life as we do, then they could do it too—just as easily!

Similarly, if we thought about our struggles the way people who have mastered them do, their success would be ours too. Just as easily.

A story is told that one of the founders of Alcoholics Anonymous was attending a session of Overeaters Anonymous. Afterward, when asked about his impressions, he said he learned you can't cross disciplines—alcoholics are alcoholics, and overeaters are overeaters.

He went on to explain why. The whole time he was listening to people struggle with food, he could only think one thought, *why don't you just stop eating*!

Even though he knew that advice is counter-productive for an alcoholic, he couldn't help himself from thinking it when it came to food.

Why? Because for him overeating was not a challenge. His thoughts and ideas allowed him to easily have self-control with food, although this was not so with alcohol.

Why is something easy for you and hard for another? Because you think about these things in ways that make it easy and they don't.

The alcoholic isn't strong when it comes to food, and thus he isn't going to conquer alcohol by trying to be strong. He just needs to think about alcohol in ways similar to which he thinks about food.

Thus, if we thought the way winners think, we would do what they do too.

People who achieve what you want to achieve are not working harder than you, they simply think about those things in ways that make it easy for them.

You can think that way too.

One of the ideas my teacher, Rabbi Noah Weinberg Ztl, used to continuously emphasize is that if you could engineer the atoms of a leaf in the right order, the leaf could blow up a city. And, those same atoms engineered correctly could be used for a nuclear power station, to power up an entire city.

All the more so, within us is enough power to blow up the entire world. Alternatively, if used correctly, we have enough energy to actually change the world for the better. When we can figure out how to channel our fullest selves, everything is attainable.

In 1954 Roger Bannister became the first person in recorded history to run the mile in under four minutes. For close to one hundred years prior people were attempting that very goal, but couldn't succeed. However, within one year of Bannister's achievement, people were running even faster than him.

Which means, those people could have done it before Bannister.

But they didn't!

Why not?

When asked about this Bannister reportedly answered, "It wasn't a physical boundary, it was a mental one." The same way my daughter was blocked about riding a bike.

What does that mean?

They had the hardware to do it, but not the software. They didn't think about the problem in a way that allowed for success.

Specifically, they didn't think they could do it.

If they had thought differently, the opportunity would have opened up for them. The proof is that when they did think differently (because of Bannister's success), they were then able to do something they previously thought impossible.

You can't do something you think you can't do.

Even if you really can!

This example is perfect to illustrate our own frustrations.

If we had the opportunity to interview one of those other runners before Bannister broke the four-minute barrier, how would they describe the obstacle they were facing?

Apart from their belief that it was impossible to run that fast, they would also profess in no uncertain terms that their effort was at its maximum—they couldn't be any tougher or find more energy and speed.

And this is the most interesting of truths.

Roger Bannister went into the history books as running the mile in 3 minutes 59.4 seconds. The person who ran that same distance in 4 minutes, just 0.6 seconds slower, was working just as hard as Bannister.

Similarly, people who achieve phenomenal results are not necessarily working harder than you. They don't have more stamina. They just have better ideas.

Ideas will transform the same effort you are now making into far better results.

The Right Idea and the Right List

Many traditions have a concept of heaven and hell.

In my tradition, heaven is the place where we will see a recording of all our accomplishments and bask in the glory of all our successes.

Alternatively, hell is the place where we see what accomplishments we could have achieved using those very same efforts. Not more work, but the same work. But because we did not understand, we missed incredible opportunities.

Imagine one of those runners realizing they could have been the first person to run the mile in under four minutes! Not by strength, but simply by thinking they could do it.

How many opportunities are we missing because we are lacking the right ideas? The opportunity is staring us in the face, but we can't see it because we don't have the right concepts.

Ideas are what allow us to achieve the remarkable. It is all there, for any one of us. All that is missing is the thinking.

"Every block of stone has a statue inside it and it is the task of the sculptor to discover it."
—Michelangelo

I am sure everyone reading this book employs a simple "to-do" list, but amazingly not too long ago such a tool was a rarity.

In 1918, Charles M. Schwab, the president of Bethlehem Steel Corporation, invited the productivity consultant, Ivy Lee, to advise his top executives. He famously suggested that before they end their day, managers list and number their top priorities for the following day. Then work on those tasks in the order of their importance as daily time allows, not proceeding until a task was completed. For this suggestion Schwab later paid Lee $25,000 (approximately $400,000 today), saying it had been the most profitable advice he had received. (Source: INC.com and James Clear)

The simple task of organizing your day around a "to-do" list increases your effectiveness dramatically, but a person who uses such a list is not better, or more endowed, than one who doesn't. It's just a simple idea that helps channel your energies in order to achieve greater results.

The person using a "to-do" list, and the one who does not, are equally motivated, but their results will vary significantly. Invariably, the one with the better ideas is often able to work less hard while achieving more.

"In fact, once you are on the right track in golf, doing things the right way takes a lot less effort than the wrong way does."
—Ben Hogan
Holder of nine golf championship titles

America is comprised of people from every other nation. At the time of this writing it is the richest and most powerful nation in the world. Its wealth, however, does not derive from natural resources, but rather from the productivity of the people living there.

What is incredible is that this wealth is achieved through the same kind of people that are in every other county. Think of it like a golf club. In my hands it's just a bent stick, but in the hands of Jack Nicklaus, Ben Hogan, or Jordan Spieth it's a magical wand. They can do things that can make you think their club is straight out of Harry Potter.

Similarly, put the average Mexican, Swede, or Englishman in the USA and they become a different person. Just like the golf club, America is able to transform people into something magical.

But it's really not a trick or a secret. When people from any country learn better ideas, they achieve far more than they would in their country of origin. These ideas include freedom of speech, equality, and justice for all.

An idea is simply a tool, a "to-do" list, or a computer. Valuing freedom of speech and the rule of law are ideas. These ideas help a nation function together in ways that allow all its citizens to achieve far more than those same people could achieve individually or in a nation not blessed with such concepts.

I can still remember when I was a little kid trying to tie one of my first pair of laced shoes and thinking how impossible it was.

I was certain that the shoes were poorly designed. I was convinced that two strings diametrically opposed to each other could never stick together.

Of course, the reality was that it was not a problem in the shoes—it was a problem with me. I didn't have the knowledge to turn the situation into a success.

This is true with every situation we face. It's the simple ideas that transform frustrating circumstances into winner moments.

The potential for great success is hidden in plain view.

Yes, the situation you are in now is frustrating, but the idea that you need to be able to solve it is easy. In fact, it's so obvious, once you see it, you will wonder how you missed it.

This is not so strange. I am sure you can look back on your life and wish you had the challenges that frustrated you ten or twenty years ago. However, at that time you didn't think they were such a breeze. Similarly, one day you will be able to look back at this juncture and see how simple the solution really was.

CHAPTER 3
Easy and Simple

One simple idea distinguishes winners from everyone else.

Winners know winners are not born.

Steve Jobs did not exit the womb with a computer chip in his mouth. Warren Buffet was not born holding a stock tip, and Thomas Edison didn't change the light bulb above his crib.

Listen carefully to what this means: *Winning is no easier or harder for you than it is for anyone else*—including the people who have succeeded.

This misnomer is as wide as it is egregious: That winners, when faced with an obstacle, no matter how large, are able to overcome it in a single stride. Hollywood is of no help here because it perpetuates the myth of the born winner in movies like Harry Potter and Star Wars.

The reality is, people who succeed greatly in life are well aware they have no advantage. The only difference is that they know it, and everyone else doesn't.

This misconception is of no small consequence—hardly anything is more emotionally overwhelming than feeling you don't have what it takes to triumph, that you aren't made to succeed.

There is probably no greater form of bullying then to tell a child they are a born loser. But the inverse, thinking that some people are born to win, is just as callous and just as debilitating. In short, if we ascribe to the belief that some people are born winners, in effect we are broadcasting that everyone else—which obviously includes children—are born losers.

ALLOW ME TO ANNOUNCE NOW: No one is born a loser. And nobody is born a winner.

If you want to win, you have to think like a winner. And everyone can do that. So read carefully, this is how winners think:

Winners know winners are not born.

If you can wake up to that concept with your coffee, you will be part of a very small group of highly successful people called winners.

No matter what overwhelming challenges you are up against, Steve Jobs, Margaret Thatcher, Theodore Roosevelt, and Jane Austen faced similar adversities. For Steve Jobs it may have been a challenging computer code, Margaret Thatcher might have had to overcome gender discrimination, and for you and I, it might be some inner demon or family struggle. But for each and every one of us, it feels equally challenging, equally unfair, and equally daunting.

The one absolute in what we call life is this: No one is born with a handicap and no one is born with an advantage.

What you think of as a hindrance is not what is holding

you back any more, or with any greater force, than anyone else. Whether it was George Washington or Andrew Carnegie, every successful person has had their share of hurdles to overcome. And, everyone could have given up just as easily as you.

There is only one variable: Some people believe winners are born, and some people believe winners are not. And that alone will explain your, and everyone else's, level of success.

Many people I explain this to mistakenly think that the children of Steve Jobs, Bill Gates, or Warren Buffett have an advantage—but that is only because they don't know their children.

Good looks, intelligence, money, yes, all those things can be inherited, but when it comes to true winning it doesn't matter who your parents are or what they did; no one has a leg up.

Why? Because winning is not a determinate of having the appropriate zip code, or even a significant yacht in the bay. Winning at life may involve having those things, and more, but having a great life can't be achieved simply through inheritance. If you don't believe me, read the biographies of the children of famous and successful people—if you can find them.

Do you know the names of Warren Buffet's, Bill Gates', or Marie Curie's children?

Not without looking it up. And that is the point. If winning really did give those children an advantage, then the world should have fifth generation Edison's, Beethoven's, and Lincoln's. Where is the great American novel from Mark Twain's descendants?

Exactly!

The reality is, Twain is more likely to have a few great, great grandchildren pumping gas than winning a Pulitzer for literature. The reason is that they, the children of Edison, Twain, or Charles Dickens, more than likely believed, against their parents' protestations, that winners are born.

Winners know that winning doesn't pass through the placenta, and the rest of humanity wants to believe it does. That goes for the children of winners too.

Why is this so important?

Believing winners are born provides you with all the permission you need to give up. Not everything, just the things that are important—and even then, not all the time, just when it gets outside your comfort zone.

If winning was really innate, if some people had the winning gene or the right DNA, then someone born a winner would have no difficulty in overcoming their obstacles. And therefore, by this definition, whoever finds an obstacle proves to themselves that they are not a winner.

I remember when Bjorn Borg tore up the court at Wimbledon in the 1970's and inspired my generation to take up tennis. Tiger Woods did the same for golf, Robin Williams for stand-up comedy, and Michael Jackson for music.

And even though we wore the same kind of tennis shoes and white shirts, our serves and volleys never whizzed the way Borg's did, ever so effortlessly.

These athletes and artists made it seem so easy that we felt their skills were innate. And, it is precisely because it was not easy for us that we came to believe we were not made to win Wimbledon.

Similarly, my first stint at stand-up comedy was in a room packed with budding enthusiasts who thought they were the next Chris Rock or Jay Leno. But by the second session, when it hit them that stand-up was actually difficult, most lost their ambition.

Winners make it *look* easy. And it is, for them. What they fail to inform you when you buy your first tennis racket, is that to win you have to find the easy.

Winners know there are two paths to every goal—the hard and the easy.

You will never win if you do the hard. You have to find the easy.

László Polgár is a Hungarian educational psychologist who studied intelligence at university. He similarly concluded that genius is made, not born. So convinced was László, that he decided to homeschool his three daughters and raise them according to his theory. His theory required that the child enjoy and desire to succeed, as opposed to it being imposed upon them.

Polgár began teaching his eldest daughter, Susan, to play chess when she was four years old. Six months later, Laszlo brought her to Budapest's chess club, a smoke-filled center crowded with elderly men, all veteran players. As she proceeded to defeat one player after the next, the astonishment and irritation became palpable. "I don't know who was more surprised, me or them," she recalls. One of the regulars laughed when he was asked to give the little girl a game. Susan was soon to erase the smile off his face when she extended her tiny hand across the board for a sportsmanlike victory shake. It was an ego-crushing gesture. (Source: *Psychology Today,* July 2005)

Many people laughed at his theory, not only because genius was (and still is) considered innate, but also because chess was (and to some degree still is) considered a man's game. It was Polgár though who had the last laugh when his daughters became the first, second, and sixth best female chess players in the world, gaining honors like the youngest grandmaster ever and first female grandmaster.

They also speak seven languages, including Esperanto.

Winners don't work harder at the task; they work hard at finding a way to enjoy that task—which will make it easy. Polgár "once found Sophia (the middle daughter) in the bathroom in the middle of the night, a chessboard balanced across her knees. 'Sophia, leave the pieces alone!' he told her. 'Daddy, they won't leave me alone!' she replied." (Sources: *Psychology Today*, "The Grandmaster Experiment," Carlin Flora, July 1, 2005)

Successful people are few and far between because only they know this simple truth: You have to find the easy.

I grew up in England, and I remember as a child asking my mother how you get to be royalty. Her answer was simple and emphatic. It was the way it was supposed to be, just like the sun rises in the morning: Some people are born to rule.

By the time I moved to the United States that conviction had waned a lot in me, so I was very surprised to encounter it again in the land of the free.

You might laugh at the English for believing the queen is entitled to rule the Empire, but I can find no explanation for why actors are accorded a level of reverence on par with the Duke of this or the Duchess of that. For an American, Tom Hanks, Meryl Streep, and Harrison Ford breathe out holy air.

I understand that when it comes to royalty, being born

to the right parent is scant proof of being a greater Homo sapiens, but is being an actor any greater a qualification? Is such a career more difficult, or nobler, than that of a social worker, nurse, or school teacher? What affords them this reverence if not an illusion that they are made of different stuff than the rest of us mere mortals?

The multitude of magazine cover stories in the average grocery store is evidence enough that society as a whole holds these people on a different plane. What you and I did on vacation only gets a few "likes" on Facebook, but when such details come from royalty and movie stars they are treated like they contain the secrets of the cosmos.

Many years ago Princess Anne, the daughter of Queen Elizabeth, had a car accident. No one was hurt, but by the news coverage it received, you would have thought Martians had just invaded.

What was most interesting and equally strange—at least to me—was the other car in the accident sold for more money than it would have if it were new, by a factor of many! People wanted the car touched by a princess. But people want the signature of Sylvester Stallone or Angelina Jolie with no less zeal.

This might come as a shock to anyone who venerates movie stars, but they were all born of a mother, all wore diapers, and all had to be burped—as did the kings and queens of Europe.

Please listen carefully: Kings don't make kings, and movie stars don't make movie stars—everyone else does that. We grant them their "holy" status because it fills a very important and universal need.

In one country the need will exhibit itself in royalty, in another in actors, and in another it could be cricket players or even sumo wrestlers. But there is a universal need to believe winners are born.

Why?

Because there is a universal need for an excuse to give up. And the best excuse is that winners don't have our struggles.

In fact, when it's phrased like that, then a person can say, "I am not really a failure at all. I could no more achieve what they achieved than a turtle can fly, or an eagle can swim. And since I was not born with the right stuff, I can't do it and it's not my fault."

"The search for someone to blame is always successful."
–Robert Half

All you have to do is think about your own struggles, and you can hear that little voice in your head that wants to let you off the hook say, "I was not made to win."

Nothing will guarantee your failure in life more than believing winners are born.

In truth, no one actually ever really gives up. They don't say the words, "I give up." What they say is, "I am not made to win this. I am not like those people who succeed."

Giving up is easy if you can find someone or something to blame, and sometimes that someone is yourself—for not being born a winner.

I am always amused that people think Superman a hero when bullets bounce off him. What bravery or courage does that require? I too would stand up to evil in a computer game. In fact, I think most people do.

I would even end poverty, ignorance, and maybe bring peace between the Sunnis and the Shiites, if I had what Superman has.

When we imagine that there are people with superhuman strength and ability, what we are really saying is: The obstacles that they conquered were only possible because they were made of steel.

We tell ourselves that unlike us, born winners do not sweat over obstacles—they always know the solution and are gifted with the right words to say in every situation. They are more than us. They are super.

"All men are created equal." What does that mean? Certainly and obviously none of us are the same size or talent. In fact, it's almost impossible to find and measure anything where we are alike.

Equal in front of the law. Yes, for sure. But I believe it means much more than that. Not least of which is that no one is born with a special advantage—the obstacles that Winston Churchill and Eleanor Roosevelt struggled with were just as hard as those I struggle with.

Let me spell it out clearly. If Amelia Earhart or Leonardo da Vinci looked at life the way most people look at life, they would have given up too! So would Oprah Winfrey, Isaac Newton, and Walt Disney.

They didn't succeed because of where they were born or how much money their parents had. They succeeded because they saw life in ways that allowed them to win, despite the obstacles that could have stopped them.

What way is that?

They didn't believe winners are born.

When you live with that idea for a while, then you know that there must be a way to make your life-goal achievable.

There must be a way to win.

This is how winners think. Whether it's Bjorn Borg or Charlie Chaplin, they made it look easy because they found a way to love it.

"The goal in life is to work hard to make things easy. An alcoholic really wants to stop drinking, so he must discover a way to make that easy. If you apply this concept to everything, success will overwhelm you and not avoid you!"

—Paul Akers
bestselling author of
2 Second Lean

CHAPTER 4

Thinking Like a Winner
Made Simple

> **"When a man knows he is to be hanged in a fortnight, it concentrates his mind wonderfully."**
> –Samuel Johnson
> Eighteenth Century English writer

Ted Leonsis is one lucky man. Not because he happens to be one of the richest men in America, but because he walked out of a plane that nearly killed him.

Actually, survival was only a small part of his luck, the message he received from that experience was the big part.

As he told me, the experience gave him a new focus. And he credits it with propelling him toward an amazing life.

One of the best examples of this type of experience is a five minute TED talk by Ric Elias, who similarly survived a crash landing on the Hudson River. Google it and you won't be disappointed.

Harsh as this sounds, there is nothing like a brush with death to help you get the point.

Anita was driving her SUV when it flipped and landed upside down in the middle of the freeway. Thankfully she and her daughter had their seat belts on, and another vehicle didn't hit them. They managed to crawl out and wait on the hard shoulder. Finally, a state trooper pulled up.

After she finished describing the whole episode to me, she added, "I hear the birds chirping, I can see colors in the trees." Her senses were kicked into overdrive and she experienced life on a whole new and incredibly meaningful level.

These three examples illustrate an interesting human phenomena: Most of the time our brains operate far less than their capability. But when we are at full speed, we experience a whole different world we simply don't normally see. These moments, typified through a brush with death, open our minds to that which we normally miss.

Put another way, the vast majority of people are walking around blind to the richness of life—that is until a near death experience shows them what they are missing.

That experience is like having a window open, and they can see new horizons of potential. It's like living life in black and white, and then one day, it's all in color.

Unfortunately, this uber-awareness also works in the opposite extreme.

On a trip to London a while ago I saw this warning label on a pack of cigarettes.

"Smoking can cause a slow and painful death."

As far as I am aware, the only other product available in a regular market with that kind of label is rat poison. Everything else emphasizes a product's benefits. Soap to make you look younger, tea to calm your nerves, and even milk to make you stronger.

It's hard to imagine an airline voluntarily displaying their

poor safety record. Or a car manufacturer posting on the windshield
how many fatalities occurred in this
model. So how do people manage to
buy something with a label declaring
their almost certain demise?

The answer is simple and brutal.
Just because an idea is true, and just
because you read it, doesn't mean you
have accepted it. It's like Ted Leonsis
before the accident—he just couldn't
access this higher awareness, even if
it was spelled out.

An example of cigarette
packaging in the U.K.

You can read it (the label on the cigarette package), you can
even nod your head in agreement, but your mind just can't
"access" it in a way that gets you to change.

These are the two extremes of life. On the low end is the inability to access a dire truth. On the high end is the new sense
of life's richness you get from a near catastrophic shock.

"Nothing in life is so exhilarating as to be shot at without result."
–Winston Churchill

At the low end of the spectrum is where the information
does not penetrate the cerebral cortex. The knowledge re-
mains external to you, even though you can read it and see it.
You just don't take it in. You don't *experience* it.

The skill of making what you read or learn *so real* that it becomes part of you is an essential key to winning. But most people find this hard to do. So we need to change that and make it easy, because, as we have been explaining, if it isn't easy, it won't happen.

This ability to change is not a talent. Rather, it is a skill. And practice makes it happen. Specifically, repeating an idea until it gets into your bones.

Anyone can watch a YouTube video on tennis moves. But the person who has a shot at Wimbledon is the person willing to practice that move over and over again until it becomes part of who they are.

Highly successful people make ideas real through repetition. And repetition.

Let's imagine for a moment having a private audience with your historical hero. Maybe it's Nelson Mandela, George Washington, or Eleanor Roosevelt.

In that meeting they divulge the secret to their success, the one idea that drove them each to greatness.

And then what?

Nothing.

Knowing their idea, just like knowing smoking kills, doesn't change anything. That is why we can read a book on Warren Buffett and never make it as an investor. We can read a book on General Patton and never be a leader of men.

Because it's not real knowledge, it's just hearing the words.

We all know why we put on weight. We all know what a lack of exercise does to us. We all know anger doesn't solve anything. We all know lots of things.

The trouble is, we don't really know.

We haven't made it *our idea*.

Unless we *really know*, unless the ideas penetrate, then all we really have is a statement. It's not real knowledge. It's like a neon sign above our head—it has no meaning except for the fact that it might be a little annoying.

You know crack cocaine is death, and the addict probably knows it too. But it's not the same knowledge. He has not internalized it.

If the addict knew it like you know it, he would stop his drug use on the dot this sentence ends with.

My father-in-law was a smoker for most of his life. No one else in his immediate family smoked, and thus everyone consistently and constantly was on his case. He knew all the statistics and read the propaganda, but nothing could get him to stop—except his four-year-old grandson (my son).

One day, when Grandpa went to pick him up, his grandson said "Grandpa you smell."

And that was it!

Not his wife, not his children, not his doctors, not the gruesome documentaries, nothing got through but this.

His grandson opened the window.

Changing is easy, that is, once you open the window and let the information in.

I have a student who was bulimic. He's a very successful businessman, family man, and an all-around good and smart guy. He knew what he was doing was dangerous and harmful to his body. But, like every addict, and every other bad habit we all engage in, the information just didn't get through.

Until that is, he saw his daughter purging.

Similarly, if you got into your bones what Warren Buffet understands in his bones, then you would achieve as much as he has. Buffet opened the window and saw what success looked like, just as Ric Elias, my father-in-law, and the bulimic did.

What's more, Buffet can tell you what he sees. In fact he tells people all the time. He is amazingly prolific and open about how to win like him. The problem is, just reading what he gets doesn't translate into us *getting it too*.

There are a multitude of expressions illustrating the experience of opening that window and getting it:

"It just clicked."

"A light bulb went on."

"Waking up to smell the coffee."

Maybe you have said these words: "I wish I knew then what I know now."

The truth is, you did know then. You had heard the words. You just didn't get the words. You didn't fully get them until they smacked you in the face. When an addict finally quits and looks back at years wasted engaged in a pointless habit, he wishes he knew then what he knows now. Clearly he did know, or at the least people close to him had told him, but being told is not the same thing as getting it.

Almost every smoker *eventually* gets to the understanding that is posted on those packs of cigarettes. Unfortunately, that understanding can sometimes happen when their doctor tells them they only have few months to live.

The trick of life is to *get* the warning label before the doctor has to spell it out for you. But it's not just a doctor, it can be your accountant telling you about your impending bankruptcy, or a police officer knocking on your door, or all kinds of terrible scenarios.

Think of this book as the warning label on the cigarettes…

but for life. This is what you want to know. Now. You don't want to come back to this book in five or ten years and say: "I wish I had gotten it then."

But how do you get these ideas *in*?

Truthfully, it doesn't take long, just the desire to know now, not later.

Watch the Ric Elias video and you'll see someone get it in less than five minutes. But outside of booking a one-way flight to a war zone on Disaster Airlines, or flipping your car on the freeway, how can we engineer this kind of awareness?

We can't easily rewrite our code—human beings are not that cognitively advanced.

This is THE CHALLENGE:

By the time you finish this book you will have read concepts that will give you the success in life you want. You will literally realize you are holding the keys to phenomenal success. You will almost certainly agree that these are the ideas to achieving a fulfilling life. But like every idea, just like the one posted on the side of a cigarette pack, they have to get in—because either the ideas get in, or the nicotine does.

Maybe you have had the experience of driving home and without paying attention ended up at your previous address. Or dialed an old telephone number. We do these things out of habit. Even though we know it's a mistake, it is nevertheless hard getting new information into our brain.

This is the point, this book was not written to tell you how to be a winner—it was written so that you will be a winner.

What's the difference?

For at least thirty years I have been on a quest: Not to teach people how to win, but teach them to be winners. I don't want you to simply read these ideas as abstract information. I want you to *live* the truly great life.

You will be a winner when you think like one.

And that will happen if you are willing to read this book again, and possibly again, until the ideas get through.

Transformation comes through absorption. Each successive reading will change you.

On your second reading you are going to be surprised. An idea will invariably stand out and will shake up the way you view life. And even though you know you read it before, nevertheless, you just didn't get it the first time around. This repetition is the process of opening the window, but doing it this way is a lot more pleasant than being on a plane that nearly crashes. Or sitting in the waiting room for the doctor to give you the prognosis.

See for yourself. If on your second reading you find yourself surprised at something you know you already read, then read it a third time and see what happens.

How many times do you have to repeat your new address before you get it? Whatever that number is, you will keep repeating it because you don't want to drive to the wrong location.

The same is true with life.

If you want to win, simply read this book again.

It's practically impossible to read this book three times and not change.

As I tell my students, return until it seems obvious—then you have changed.

Part 2

CHAPTER 5

The Three Most Important Days of Life

Tomorrow, today, and yesterday.

To be precise, it's not specifically tomorrow, but how you think about the future that counts.

The same goes for the present and the past. It's all in how you think about them.

But make no mistake—this idea is epic.

Your daily life is shaped by these three concepts. And they are your absolute source for motivation, enthusiasm and, not least, resolve.

When done right, exquisitely right, a human being can perform at levels commonly considered heroic. But in truth, all they are doing is what we can all do: Using these three days properly.

I should note, and you need to be aware, that when these three days are approached incorrectly they will inflict immense pain and inner turmoil.

Human beings are built in such a way that we think about the future, the present, and the past in very distinct and powerful ways.

The future is a massive tractor-beam type of force that pulls on our disposition all the time. Events far in the future have a profound effect on us right now, in the present.

Our ability and, crucially, our inability to ignore the future will dictate much of our mood in the present. What you think will happen in one week, and even in one decade, intensely influences your temperament in the present.

Imagine for a moment you just found out you won the lottery. Even though you don't actually have the money in hand, nevertheless, anticipating a huge check in the near future changes your current attitude. How you foresee your future life will inescapably affect your attitude in the present.

Let me explain how significant an idea this is. Try and picture how you would really feel if you found out you won the jackpot. How would it affect your mood if a text came through right now declaring you the big winner?

I think it's fair to say that upon hearing such good fortune most people would find themselves in extreme exuberance. And, in that kind of mood, your performance levels would shoot through the roof. Negativity vanishes and new opportunities spring up like frogs, all simply because of your great new attitude. People you used to find annoying become irrelevant, even amusing. Inhibitions often vanish, and previous obstacles fall.

One of the greatest periods in American productivity occurred during World War II. This was without sensitivity training, ambient music, adjustable chairs, or profit-sharing schemes. Why? Because there was a shared vision of a great future.

The expectation of a great future is the easiest, and in all

reality, the only way to consistently boost personal or business productivity.

Now appreciate what we have just come to realize. The difference between *how you actually feel right now*, and *how you would feel* if you anticipated a great future, is no small gap.

Therefore, the reason your mood and level of engagement is what it is, is because your vision of your future is not bright enough (or at least not as bright as winning the lottery) to allow you to be the best you can be. All that positive energy is still in there, it's just dormant. You are leaving a lot of yourself on the table because you just don't have a big enough vision for your future.

Simply put, whatever you are predicting your future to be, is creating your mood, disposition, and effectiveness right now. If that future is wonderful, then your mood is wonderful. If you think your future is bland, so too your mood. And even worse, predicting a miserable future is obviously a big downer.

Therefore, you cannot be the great person you are destined to be without a great future in mind.

We are what we think the future will bring.

We are our future.

But don't ignore your past.

Although, the truth is, you can't ignore it, because each person's unique history dictates much of their daily activity.

The past plays a heavy hand in our present, just like the hand hidden behind a puppet. It's written all over our faces, and in everything we do.

But as interesting as your past might be, it's not as important as how you think about that past.

This is somewhat complicated, so allow me to explain.

Twins, with almost an identical history, can nevertheless perform at vastly different levels because of how they view that past. If they both have the same thing happen to them, but one views it positively and the other negatively, the way they behave will dramatically change.

Animals, especially wild animals, live in the present; we don't.

A lion hunts a gazelle pretty much the same way as every other lion no matter how they were raised. The same goes for monkeys climbing trees and salmon swimming upstream. No matter what their individualized history may have been, they really live and perform in the present as though the past did not happen.

It doesn't mean that an animal's past does not affect their present. Obviously, an abused dog or a dog missing a limb is going to behave differently, but where they differ from people is that an animal doesn't *ponder* their past in a way that changes their present. We do.

Animals don't anguish, agonize, and imagine a different or better past. Our past invades our present actions and thinking, to the point that it shows up in almost everything we do, wear, eat, and speak.

How many times have we walked out of our house to look up at a glorious sky, and yet the only thing our mind can focus on was yesterday's tragedy? A person can have a completely picture-perfect day, yet fail to enjoy a single moment of it because of their past. The past is as real today as it was when it happened.

As such, it is impossible to live in the present and ignore the past or future. What we can, and thus should do, is manage those two forces (past and future) so that we can make the present the best it can be.

These two imposing forces, the past and the future, are like the shrinking sides of a trash compactor, and can easily override anything happening in the present. In the extreme it's easy to witness—you probably know people who are plagued by nightmares from their childhood. And there are others who can't concentrate on anything because they are anticipating some dire news. Abuse from the past, or disease and financial stress clouding the future, are two vampires that suck the life out of our present.

To understand this better, make a simple list of your biggest aggravations—things you are worried about, grieving about, and struggling with, from the small to the massive—by writing each annoyance in its appropriate box below. A relative who ripped you off a few years ago goes in the past, even though you have to see him today. A customer who is giving you a hard time goes in the present box. And the mortgage that is due tomorrow goes in the future. Fill the boxes with everything that is of concern, and then sit back.

THE PAST	THE PRESENT	THE FUTURE

What you should notice is that even though the events described may span decades, from an early childhood memory to an upcoming deadline, they nevertheless all seem to crowd today. It's as though the past and the future are right here, right now.

The other thing you should notice is each box has a different flavor to it. The events in the *past box* affect your determination or resolve. The *present box* is very much tied to your excitement and joy for the day. And the *future* is going to dampen motivation.

What I want you to know is this: It doesn't need to be this way.

What we are going to explain is that without changing or removing anything from those boxes—except how you think about them—you can create, or recreate, a phenomenal life.

The common mistake is in thinking that some people are fortunate that they don't have anything in those aggravation boxes. And that is why they are so successful. *But this is clearly not the case.*

What we are going to see is this: Highly successful people, what we are calling winners, have had exactly the same, and in some cases worse, experiences. *It's not what happens to you that counts.* What does count is thinking about your experiences in ways that make your life great—and winners know just how to do that.

Remember, they weren't born with it, they *learned* how to do it. And you can learn it too.

We are going to change the way you think in such meaningful ways that those aggravating events are going to transform into incredibly positive sources of energy.

I know that sounds like a very tall order, so stay tuned!

Louis Zamperini, Olympic distance runner, World War II hero, and the subject of a major Hollywood movie (*Unbroken*), had plenty of abuse in his history, not least of which were two years in a Japanese POW camp where he suffered disease, starvation, and near-daily beatings.

But it wasn't until later in Zamperini's life that his past experience became so consuming it almost broke him, something that his guards could not achieve.

Notice this very human phenomena: When the torment was in the present, Zamperini could resist, but when it became his past it became unbearable. Just because you can overcome an obstacle in the present does not mean you will be similarly capable when it becomes your history.

As I said above, when we don't think about any one of the time frames correctly they become the cruelest of jailors.

This is therefore a crucial point: We cannot deal with the past in the same way we deal with the present or future.

Zamperini had to learn what you too can learn: Managing the past correctly will transform a burden into an inspiration.

I am sure nearly every person reading this book is dogged by some kind of past malice. Very, very few people are free from such resentments.

So please note Louis Zamperini's lesson.

When he made two trips to Japan to reconcile with his former captors, he embraced many of those who came forward. However, the infamous Mutsuhiro Watanabe—Zamperini's cruel and sadistic tormentor—refused to meet his former captive.

While Zamperini transformed his past into an empowering and awe-inspiring life, Watanabe could not. He could not face his history and thus, inevitably, his life ended in insignificance.

Abuse is a large rock to climb out from under, but the abuser is faced with an even more formidable mountain to overcome. Although I have seen many an abused soul redeem the suffering they had experienced, I have yet to meet an abuser who has done likewise. I am not saying it's impossible, I have heard stories of people who did just that. I am just saying that of the two, the abused has it easier. *Not easy, just easier.*

The reason we find this so counterintuitive is because we believe the abuser has a choice and the abused does not. But this is not true, the abuser or the bully is trapped in a blind maze of distorted thinking that his happiness will only come through the suffering of others (King Solomon, Proverbs 4:16). But when he finally runs out of lives to destroy he is going to have a very hard time facing what he has done. And unless he does actually face it, he will never realize where true happiness is.

An abuser is like a dead person—just like a dead person is unaware, so too an abuser can't comprehend the pain they have inflicted. As such, they are dead to the feelings of others.

I know suffering abuse is horrendous. I never want to minimize that suffering. But of the two, I would rather be the abused than the abuser.

Being oblivious to the pain of others is not a better way to live! Happiness, love, friendship, community, and companionship are the expensive, and certainly worthwhile luxuries of life. But too many people live in the poverty of these delicacies because they are too cheap and miserly to pay the price of remorse and acknowledge that they are the cause of another's pain.

When you admit you have caused someone pain, you are making a bold, brave, and noble statement: "I don't want my foolish actions to get between us and ruin our love and friendship."

However, let me be clear here. It is impossible to live with other people and not offend and hurt them. It's just impossible. Human beings are way too sensitive to not be easily slighted and hurt (usually often). And as such you can be sure you have offended the people you live with. If you don't believe me, surprise yourself and ask them, and you will surely be taken aback by their answer. Be sure to mention to them that you *really* want to know. Most people are too reserved to tell the truth on this.

Thus, our past is a powerful force. And, just like electricity or even nuclear energy, it can be very destructive—*very self-destructive.*

Alternatively, if you tame and channel that past, it will give you all that you need to lead a winning life.

Your history absolutely does not matter. It only matters how you *think* about that history. It's not your past that is holding you back; it's only the way you think about that past. No matter what your past, no matter how bad you think it was, you can use it to be the person you want to be. It has all the propulsion you need to become the winner you are built for.

Zamperini's experience is extreme, but the thinking is the same. Successful people have simply figured out what kind of thinking goes with what kind of day. And the rest of us have not. The right attitude toward your past and future allow you to live in the present like nothing else will.

I am sure as you are reading this book your brain is sending you messages about your future. Impending meetings and crises you have to deal with are flashing across your mind's screen. On top of that, past experiences and regrets have probably been triggered, to such a degree that the present hardly exists. If we don't properly manage them, then the past and future become merciless jailors of our present lives.

How we *should* think about either one of these time periods is not how most people *actually* do think about them. Obviously we think about the past, present, and future, but most of us simply don't think of them in ways that produce the life we want. Nearly everyone has mixed one with the other, and when we do that we get very little done, or worse.

I am sure all this sounds somewhat odd and bizarre. It may be hard to imagine how else to think about the past, but please bear with me as we explore and explain some simple ideas that will revolutionize your thinking.

This is a bigger insight than most people appreciate because thinking about the past is so natural to us. We assume we are thinking about it correctly. The same applies to the present and future.

But what if you don't? What if you are thinking about these three time frames incorrectly?

What we are going to see is that most people get it wrong. Badly.

Almost certainly all of your frustration—and especially your frustration with others—is in thinking about the past, present, and future in ways that don't match the appropriate periods.

It's like a calculator company that uses software from a different manufacturer. Invariably it is not going to work, at least not well. So too a person, just like a calculator, has to match the hardware with the right software to get to full functionality, and any deviation is going to create varying degrees of miscalculations.

There is so much more we are capable of than what we are experiencing and actualizing now.

In the next few chapters we are going to explain how you have all the resolve you need—it's waiting for you in your past. Enthusiasm is in your present, and motivation will be found in your future.

Let's open up that world.

CHAPTER 6
The Meaning of Life

Picture the absolute best day of your life. The kind of day they make movies out of.

It can be one that actually happened, or one you imagine.

It's a blow-the-roof-off kind of day with the passion and energy to power a medium-sized city for a year.

We've all had days like that. Perhaps it was an event or achievement that made you feel so amazing—maybe something you bought, like a dream house in Patagonia.

Maybe it has to do with another person. It could be a graduation, or something you overcame. Your first car, or the last vacation you took.

If it will help you get into the mood, imagine a genie popping out of a bottle with three grand wishes. You can be as unrealistic and imaginative as you want.

Take as long as you need and give it lots of details. If you really want to get the most out of this exercise, write it all down and elucidate with examples and personal experiences; or just go ahead and employ pure fantasy.

The more time you give to this exercise, and more importantly, the more real you make it feel, the more impact this tool is going to have on your life. Give yourself all the time you need before reading on.

Now take a deep breath and go back in your mind to the worst experience of your life. On this one, don't invent anything that didn't really happen to you. Take a real bottom-of-the-barrel example from your personal life.

Obviously, this is a bit of a downer—I apologize, but this exercise is key to understanding what your life is all about.

And it's important that you actually go through these steps, and not just read the words and nod.

Okay, now that you have done these exercises, let's put the two experiences together.

This is what you need to imagine:

You are in the middle of that best day, having an incredibly good time. But, for whatever reason, you know what is coming. . . .

The worst day.

And it's coming next week.

And even though you know it's coming, there is nothing you can do to stop it.

You only know what it is, and that it's going to happen.

So, how is that best day working for you now?

If you have been playing along, what you should experience is a complete deflation. That best day that you were imagining has little or no value whatsoever.

What does all this mean?

This is the lynchpin.

It doesn't matter what kind of day you are having today. It

only matters what kind of day you think you are going to have tomorrow, or next week, or next year.

You could be one of the richest people on this planet.

You could be one of the most well respected personalities alive.

You could also be the CEO of one of the most admired companies in the world.

But on the day Steve Jobs (who had all the above) is informed he has only three months to live, he is having a very bad day.

People think (mistakenly) that if they are having a good day, then they are having a good day.

The problem is, they aren't.

There is no such thing as having a good day if tomorrow isn't good.

How you *think* about your future *makes* your present.

It matters very little what today is. It only matters what you think tomorrow is going to be.

Take a person who is a total contradistinction to Steve Jobs: He is absolutely penniless and truly pitiful. All this guy owns is the ragged shirt on his back. He is emaciated, weighing only eighty pounds and it's hard to tell if he is even alive because his breathing is barely perceptible.

If that is not bad enough, his whole family is dead or murdered.

But it's 1945, and he has just been informed that the Allies have won the war, and his camp, Auschwitz, has just been liberated.

And that is the day that will be remembered by him as the best day of his entire life!

Why?

Because his future is so much brighter than his present.

It doesn't matter what today is—it only matters what you think tomorrow is going to be.

It doesn't matter if you are having a good day. Or, to be more accurate, you can't have a good day today unless you think tomorrow (the future) is going to be good.

Today does not make today good, only tomorrow does.

In other words, there is no such thing as having a good day. Searching for one is as pointless as looking for dragons or fairies at the end of the garden.

Our experience will testify that knowing tomorrow is going to be awful will inevitably, and absolutely, make a perfectly fine today awful too.

As such, it is practically impossible to win the lottery and be depressed—even though at the very moment of winning not one iota of your life has actually changed. It's the thought that the future is going to be better that lifts your spirits now.

You still have all the same financial and personal issues, right now. But everything changes today when you know that in a fairly short amount of time you will be able to solve those issues. At least you think you will.

Similarly, if a person thinks tomorrow is going to be really ghastly it is impossible to change their spirits today, no matter how much you improve their condition.

People who succeed in astounding ways are faced with the same obstacles that you face, sometimes more. However, they understand this fundamental and universal truth of existence: You will have a great day today if you expect an amazing one tomorrow.

In sum, you can't have a great life without great expectations. This concept of tomorrow is going to have profound consequences in your life, and it will bring the other two time frames—the present and the past—together. A great future allows you to enjoy the challenges of today, as well as learn the lessons of yesterday.

Imagine you are on your way to work when the news on the radio blares out that the economy has tanked and every type of business is under stress. Then, your best friend in management calls to tell you that the company you both work for is about to go bankrupt.

Alternatively, switch that out for this scenario: Your company has just been bought out by Amazon.com and that same friend messages you to rush to work because upper management is going to give you a big promotion.

In both of these cases, your workload that day is going to feel very different, even though it's the same work.

If you know tomorrow is going to be fantastic, it's so much easier to think about, and deal with, the struggles you are facing today in far more productive ways.

Before a battle, the generals on both sides give their troops a pep talk, but the one who can convince his troops that victory is imminent has the edge. Same weapons, same territory, but the soldier who believes he is going to win fights with more passion.

It's how winners think. That they are going to win.

You can think that way too!

CHAPTER 7
Control Freaks Rejoice!

It's time to come out of denial. We are all control freaks! Human beings simply love being in control.

Even people who claim to not have any control issues, at some point had to overcome them. Because we all have an innate need that things work out the way we would like. I believe everyone would choose more control if it helped.

Consider babies and small children: They like getting their way and don't react well when they don't. Parents have to painstakingly educate their progeny to the fact that all options are not on the table—much to the child's chagrin.

Most people learn that they simply cannot control the outcome, at least not always. Even though those outcomes are sometimes very important to us.

And some people don't learn.

We've all met those people.

But maybe there is a third alternative.

Control is really our desire to make a difference, and we all need things to turn out well. Therefore, trying to quell the need to control is emotionally unhealthy. A far better way is to effectively use this need to win.

Control will mess us up when we try to control that which we can't. But instead of abandoning the idea of control, we need to use it for those things we can control.

What we can control is the future, and it's the only place control works well.

Let me explain with an example.

A student of mine described to me how she had used the ideas from our class to get out of paying a ticket.

Since paying parking tickets is a pet peeve of mine, I was all ears.

The police had towed her parked car, and to add insult to injury, she had actually parked legally! The police had made a mistake.

When she went down to the impound lot to collect her car, she told her story to the duty officer, who upon checking the details, corroborated her claim.

"Okay," he told her, "when you pay the fine ask the lot attendant for the telephone number to claim back your money."

"Pay the fine!" she exclaimed. "You towed me inappropriately. Why do I have to pay a fine?"

The effortless way his answer flowed from his mouth indicated that this was not the first time he had dealt with this issue.

"No one takes their car out of the impound lot without paying the fine. Sorry lady, that's the law!"

Resigned to her fate, she followed his directions and reluctantly paid the fine. And as she was signing the stub, she dutifully asked for the number to call for the refund.

"Oh, no," the attendant said. "You can't get your money back."

My annoyed student replied "But you don't understand, I was inappropriately towed."

"No, you don't understand," came the stern reply. "You aren't getting your money back. The guy in charge is the most miserable human being you'll ever meet. His only joy in life is the power he yields denying people their claims."

Undeterred, she made up her mind. She was going to get her money back! And the ideas she had just learned were the key.

She called the number, and as to be expected Mr. Control Freak allowed her the time to make her claim—which, she knew, he would deny so he could get his one little piece of perverse pleasure.

So, after an exhaustive recounting of the pertinent story, she added this little tidbit at the very end:

"You probably don't have the power to grant me a refund, so could you tell me who does?"

She got her money back.

My student knew Mr. C. needed to feel he had control, so she set it up in such a way that he could only show it by giving her a refund.

You have probably heard the expression, "power corrupts and absolute power corrupts absolutely." I would like to suggest that's not quite accurate.

It's really the need to control the present that messes us up. Absolutely and always. And the more you try to control, the greater the mess.

Mr. C.'s desire for control was his undoing. And it is ours, too. That is if our need to control is in the present.

Let me explain some more.

As we have mentioned, human beings have a deep need to feel in control. That need is not going to go away—it can only be channeled. If it's in the present it creates all kinds of social, personal, and even business dysfunctions, as the previous example showed.

You simply can't control the present. Life never goes the way you think it should. I am sure as you are reading this book there are a number of things, just today, that you are disappointed about.

That is because the essence of life is unpredictability. It's what life is all about. We live in an existence that is fundamentally unpredictable—and we don't like it one bit!

We like the predictable, but life loves the spontaneous.

"Quantum particles do not behave like tennis balls . . . To get from one place to another, they take all the possible paths in space and time . . . The particle . . . literally went everywhere. Simultaneously."
—Christophe Galfard
*The Universe in Your Hand: A Journey
Through Space, Time, and Beyond*

Look at nature. Spontaneity is built into the system. Animals constantly adapt to the situations they find themselves in. The slightest noise or abnormality sends a rabbit or bird in a completely different direction. In a blink of an eye they are gone. To survive and succeed in life, a life has to be able to change.

That ability to adapt to a new situation doesn't exist in human beings on the physical level. We are sorely lacking the agility to react effectively on a dime. On the mental level, however, we can be remarkably adept with the things life throws at us.

That starts by realizing we can't control the present.

If you want the present to be what you think it should be, then you will be one of those watching the last lifeboats leave the Titanic. The more a person tries to control the present, the more they are unable to adapt.

Life has no time for wishful thinking about what your day should have been. That's what it means to live in the present.

And so, paradoxically, by trying to control the present a person becomes controlled by what happens to them.

Golf is a most instructive example of this concept. Ben Hogan, the same golf great as quoted in Chapter 2, said, "Not even the best golfer can hit the ball this well on every shot, for golf, in essence, is a game of misses."

Hogan is making a remarkable point. The ball is stationary, the golfer is an expert, and all he has to do is what he has trained years to do. There are no unpredictable variables like a pitcher or a moving target, and yet each swing creates an unpredictable result.

Even when we reduce an activity to a set of knowns, we will still end up with an unknown; and all the more so with the rest of life, which is far more fluid.

Life abhors the predictable.

> **"One of the most curious consequences of quantum physics is that a particle like an electron can seemingly be in more than one place at the same time until it is observed, at which point there seems to be a random choice made about where the particle is really located."**
> —Marcus du Sautoy
> *The Great Unknown: Seven Journeys to the Frontiers of Science*

Whatever you thought today was going to be, *it wasn't*. And importantly, it never will be.

An excellent example of this is a wedding. I have been to many, many weddings, and despite the fact that professionals are organizing a cookie cutter event with months and months of planning, invariably and almost always, things don't go according to plan.

I once took a course in stand-up comedy. Why?

After a speech, I noticed that people would come up to me and tell me how much they enjoyed it. But when I asked them what they liked, more often than not they remembered the joke.

I ruminated on this for a bit, then realized, "If it's the joke they remember, then maybe the way to make an impact is to make the message funny."

Thus the stand-up comedy course.

I learned a lot from that experience. As a group, stand-up comedians tend to be very genuine, warm people. It's hard to be funny and callous. You have to like people if you want to make them laugh.

But interestingly, I also noticed that more than a few stand-up comedians have drug or alcohol problems. I don't want to besmirch a whole category, so I am not saying it's even most of them; it just seems to have a fairly high occurrence.

Why? The pressure is enormous on entertainers. And of all entertainers, the ones who are under the most pressure are stand-up comics. In every other career your success and evaluation are based on a large number of factors over a long period of time. You might mess up once or twice, but to really destroy your career you have to ignore the warning signs for a very long time.

But a comedian's whole career is dependent on five minutes. He or she does nothing all day except wait and prepare for those five minutes. And if the guy before them bombed, if there is a national tragedy, or everyone is in a really bad mood, the comedian is sunk.

And even if everything goes their way, just as Ben Hogan said with golf, sometimes the words just don't come out right. No matter how much they prep.

There is a lot at stake, and it all boils down to a few minutes with nothing and nobody to help you out. Therefore the desire to control is hard to ignore.

But this is what I learned: If you want to be good at stand-up, you have to walk out on that stage and just relax. You simply can't control what is about to happen. And if you try, you just tie yourself up into a very tight knot.

And this is what winners do.

Whether its business, family, or stand-up comedy, *they don't try to control the present.*

If you look closely, the great comedians feel as comfortable on a stage with a mike as you and I do in our living room—they aren't faking it, they really are at home. You can't win and control the present.

You have to be at home with your slippers on. **You have to be at home in life.**

We can't control the present, and the more anyone tries the more nervous and frustrated they get. Sometimes even to the point of severe dysfunction.

But as was said at the beginning of the chapter, our need for control has to be managed. Therefore, what to do with it?

The only thing that is firmly 100 percent in our control is the future.

But how do we control the future?

How can we possibly predict what tomorrow will bring?

Let me start by pointing out something fundamental about human beings: The future is what we do.

And it is what we do best.

The future is where we can dream and plan and ponder how it should all play out.

This is not an *Alice in Wonderland* fairy tale fluffy naïve whim. This is mission-statement military-grade high-end optimization stuff. This is Steve Jobs put-a-dent-in-the-universe stuff.

Steve Jobs achieved what he did precisely because he took control of the future.

"The best way to predict the future is to create it."
—Peter Drucker
The founder of modern business management
and author of over 25 books

If your life isn't rocking, the reason is simple and plain: Your future is all messed up.

This is what your future needs to look like: Take the lessons from the past, add in the incompletes of today, and then plot out how you are going to end up whole and successful.

Tomorrow is for planning. And the range available to you is the rest of your life. You have as much space as you need to plan your life and make it as grand as you can imagine.

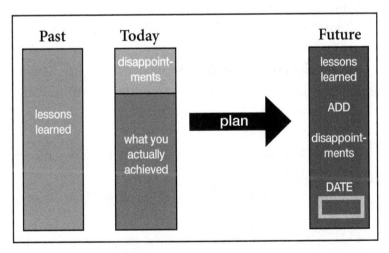

Set a date and plot a chart until you get to what you want.

This process puts you in control. And in this context, control is as healthy as smiling, which is why we are all built with this need—it's just that fulfilling this need can only happen in the future.

This is not as strange as we might first think. We all left school with dreams as big as mountains. We had big plans of what we were going to do, see, visit, and achieve. But slowly, slowly, slowly it got whittled down to a very simple goal: To have a nice day!

I am here to tell you this: *If your picture of your future is not brighter than your past, nothing can possibly make you have a great day today.*

When we plan right and establish real, exciting and gut grabbing goals, then we become innately and unbelievably motivated. This is how you get things done. This is how to think and live like a winner.

Winners chart out the path to the Promised Land. They dream big.

I know I am making it all sound so easy, but that is because it really is.

The problem is not in making great and inspiring goals, the problem is that it's more enticing to create uninspiring and mediocre goals instead.

Why do people do that?

Because they want to avoid disappointment, they settle for what people call "realistic" goals.

But this is the truth: Any goal that is realistic is never, ever going to excite you.

In 1776 the British were *the* super power of the world. They had the relative power of the combined forces of America, Russia, and China today.

George Washington could never have been motivated to

take on that giant if not for an even grander vision of what America could be. When he described how he was going to take on the superpower of the day I am sure many people told him to be more realistic.

But could President Kennedy have inspired the world with anything less than the moon? Kennedy himself admitted that they did not have the technology to pull it off. Similarly John Adams and Thomas Jefferson knew that there was a huge gap between what they had and what they needed to succeed. But to be *inspiring*, it has to be unrealistic.

Interestingly, the British knew what America's founding fathers knew as well. Their mistake, as is the mistake whenever your enemy is fighting with more inspiration than ability, was in attacking their ability instead of shrinking the inspiration.

America and their allies defeated one of the greatest threats to civilization in World War II, yet were greatly humbled by an insignificant military power in Southeast Asia. In the first conflict, America was inspired, and in the other, North Vietnam was.

Your unrealistic goals can be as big as you want, as long as they are equally inspiring.

The bigger the goal, the bigger the inspiration—the greater the life.

Personally, I would rather have an outlandish goal that was exciting than a realistic goal that was boring. At this point in my life I can look back at many a goal unmet, but I wouldn't give up going after any one of them. It's not the goals that were important—it's the striving for them that has given me such a rich life.

I have lost count of how many times I have planned on taking the world by storm. Amongst close friends it's a bit of an in-joke, "the rabbi and his plans."

But each plan has taught me incredible lessons, while also helping me learn how to define and plot the future. And, the best reward of all, is that they have given me an unbelievable life along the way.

Let me tell you about one particular goal, maybe not the most noble or earth shattering, but nevertheless one that proved to be quite eventful.

When we bought our current house I wanted to build a treehouse in our backyard. I have no idea what came over me, but I saw the tree and it said to me, treehouse!

That treehouse became a very expensive project. I burnt through many a power tool putting it all together. A number of friends joined in, I believe for no other reason than they felt sorry for me. During this time, I also became good friends with the physician at the local emergency room.

It took way too long to complete, and eventually it all had to be torn down because it became a bit of a hazard. But, and this is key, I would do it all again. The process was a thrill.

When we are firmly engaged in a great goal, it engages and enthuses the present. We wake up early and get tons done. We live on the edge and love it.

I am sure Helen Keller, Louis Pasteur, and Walt Disney had a great ride of a life too. But that life was not because of what they achieved, it was because of what they *tried* to achieve.

"I find my greatest pleasure, and so my reward, in the work that precedes what the world calls success."
—Thomas A. Edison

It isn't the success that is worth the effort, it's what happens leading up to that success.

Everyone can have that when they shoot for what they think is beyond their reach.

Pick a date, far enough in the future that it gives you room, and ask yourself, "By this date what would I love to become or achieve?"

You don't even have to try, just post it on your desk. Just the thought of it will stir your imagination and start the engines of excitement.

It's unfortunate that disappointment often makes people bitter. But why should this be? A great goal is like a roller coaster. Does anyone complain that a roller coaster lets you off where you got on, no closer to anywhere you want to be?

The reason you took the ride is not for the destination, but the journey. A magnificent goal gives you a great journey.

Isn't having a great journey what it's all about?

I have always found it strange that people feel sorry for me when I fail. Don't they know I already got my reward in trying?

Don't get me wrong. I am not suggesting you commit to a life of failure by seeking exciting but unattainable goals. Rather, the point is this: When you seek exciting goals, you achieve so much more along the way.

If you want to have a great day today, if you want to live the best life you can, if you want to be a winner, then plan your future. Big. And everything else will fall into place.

The future is where the living is.

CHAPTER 8
The Present

There is an old joke about a Wall Street trader who walks into a bar, pulls up a seat, and orders a large stiff drink over which he discharges his tale of woe.

After a fair number of these "tonics," he gets up to leave, but before exiting he orders one last one "for the road."

He quickly downs it and then, in a fit of rage, hurls the glass at the bartender, who barely dodges the projectile. Inevitably the glass smashes against the back mirror, fractures and falls, making a ferocious noise and an equally impressive mess.

The bartender is justifiably furious, but our trader crumples in shame. "I am so dreadfully sorry," he whimpers. "Please tell me how much it will cost to repair this inexcusable behavior?"

With the bartender's temper sufficiently assuaged, he takes out a piece of paper and starts calculating. Eventually he proclaims, "Three thousand bucks."

The man immediately writes out a check for $5,000 and gives it to the bartender, noting, "I added a little something for your troubles."

Six months later our trader finds himself in the same position, physically and emotionally.

Again, he orders his last drink and again hurls the glass at the bartender. And again proclaims his shame and immediately writes out a check for $5,000.

This time, though, the bartender responds: "Mister, I don't know what is going on with you, but it's not worth it to me. I don't want to see you in here again until you've been cured."

The man nods and says, "I understand, I need therapy. I promise to get it."

Six months later the trader shows up again at the bar. The bartender is a little surprised and asks, "Are you okay?"

The man says, "Yes, I went to get help like you said, and I am cured."

"Wow," replies the bartender, "in that case, the first drink is on me."

However, a dozen drinks later as the man is about to leave he orders his one more for the road. And, once again, hurls the glass at the back of the bar.

"But, you said—!?" the bartender proclaims in shock.

"I am cured" the man replies. "I don't feel bad anymore!"

Feelings of guilt, blame, and resentment are not easy emotions to rid oneself of. That's why they are the grist of many a therapist's practice.

What this book is suggesting is a very different approach to tackling these very sticky feelings.

Think of the past like a giant water balloon, hundreds of feet across, weighing multiples of tons. The only thing that can stop it from crushing you is something of commensurate weight, say another balloon of equal dimensions. That balloon is the present. If your present is equally massive, then it won't allow the past and its regrets to invade.

It's not about being busy for the sake of busyness, which is a very flawed approach. Being busy just to keep your disturbing memories at bay is no way to live. Rather, it's about living an absolutely engaging life so there is no room for regrets.

Can you remember a time when you lived like that? You might have to go back in your memory banks to your school years, or the days leading up to marriage; having your first child, or starting a business or new job.

When something utterly engages you, then your past is simply and easily kept out from infringing and ruining your present. It doesn't take effort to keep resentments out. You don't have to repeat a mantra or engage in any degree of denial.

When you are living life in the present, there is only one thing you want from the past: Its lessons.

Most of the deaths in World War I's Battle of the Somme occurred within fifteen minutes of the first day. By the end of that day the British had lost nearly 50 percent of their 120,000 troops; some being killed, others wounded or captured. The British, in their official history wrote, "There is more to be learnt from ill-success—which is, after all, the true experience—than from victories, which are often attributable less to the excellence of the victor's plans than to the weakness or mistakes of his opponent." (Source: *Elegy: The First Day on the Somme* by Andrew Roberts, quoting from *Official History of the Great War* by Sir James Edmonds).

We understand this so well in science. The people tasked with sending humans to the moon knew that even with the best of intentions, there would be a lot of trial and error. And because the goal was so consequential they therefore had to regard the past as a sponge. Meaning, the only possible way of minimizing failure is to suck out every last drop of error that is to be learned.

It was very clear that they were not going to build a better rocket without learning from the previous one; and they knew that the next one would not be as good as the one after that.

People who plot a great future do not have time for guilt because they have too much on their daily plate to add a dollop of blame or resentment. In other words, feelings of guilt and resentment are luxuries in which winners cannot afford to indulge.

The consistent mistake we make is thinking that we can be at peace with the past without having an astounding present.

This is true from another perspective as well. When you have an engaging present, when your mission today requires "All hands on deck," then you only want the lessons of the past, and nothing else.

Therefore, feelings of resentment have less to do with any indiscretion committed against us, but more to do with our lack of focus on the task at hand today.

And so, when a person slows down their daily activity, it will invariably be matched by an equal amount of resentments from their past.

This is not the way of winning. People who win aren't whining about past deals and failures; they've got too much on their present plate.

But it's even more than that.

Winners don't gripe about the past because it's precisely the lessons of that past that are helping them now. They don't resent what others did to them, because they are able to learn from it and use that lesson to propel them in the present and future. They are no more likely to have resentments against those who ripped them off than they are to the people who went out of their way to help them.

I can honestly tell you, if you get any value out of this book you need to thank my adversaries probably more than my friends—it is they who have taught me some of the most profound lessons of life.

But, when we avoid the opportunities in the present, blame and resentment from some past event will assert itself.

One single misstep from a friend or relative can cause immeasurable emotional pain that can last for years.

We may think it's the relative who is causing the pain, but it isn't.

Yes, the relative may be guilty, but you are being consumed with pain and anguish because of choices you are making today.

In my career I have had the pleasure of meeting an incredible number of diverse people. I can't think of any specific type of person I have not encountered. I have heard amazing stories and learned about extraordinary lives. And, this is what I have come to realize: Everyone has been abused.

Everyone.

Some more than others, and some in unspeakable ways. The difference between them is not the degree, but how much they let it invade and destroy their present.

A few years ago I met a Mengele twin. (The normal adjectives to describe evil people don't apply to Mengele. The hor-

ror he inflicted is still not fully appreciated because it's so far
off the scale of what people can hear. There is the Holocaust,
and then there is Mengele.) One of the unspeakable things
Mengele did was to perform brutal medical experiments on
twins.

None of that however was on the face or in the conversa-
tions of this very gentle and sweet man, one of the twins.

People's resentments from things in their past have nothing
to do with the degree of egregiousness. The inconsequential
things, along with the massive ones, will destroy your life just
as equally, and just as ruthlessly, if you don't engage life in the
present.

We can either try to change the present or we will end up
trying to change the past. When we change the present we
feel engaged in life itself. Alternatively, blame is the feeling we
have when we engage (fruitlessly) in trying to change the past.

I am sure these words sound strange indeed, "change the past."

But, as strange as these words are, our emotions believe it
is possible.

Emotions don't operate in the realm of logic. They make us
feel the past is as real as the present, and that we can just as
easily change either one.

If it were possible, the person who is engulfed in resentments and blame would hop into a time machine and change
what happened. In fact, the emotion of blame believes you
really can.

This mistake is easily observable in others. I am sure you know
more than a few people who bitterly complain about the many
injustices committed against them, whether real or imagined.
But please notice this, they all talk in the same tone, as though

the injustice had just happened and that there is something they can do about it. It's as though the past is really happening now.

What's more, they all exhibit the same pathology—a complete lack of any serious activity in the present. In colloquial terms, they don't have a job, at least not one that challenges them. People who are gainfully employed, and love their work, don't have time to moan.

Thus, it's not injustices long gone that create a person's emotional turmoil today, no matter how much they claim it is. It's their lack of present problems or present activity that brings out their past grudges.

As such, resolving the past won't solve anything in a person's life. But finding serious and engaging work will. Even seriously trying to find a job will do the trick.

A passenger on the Titanic has every right to hold a deep grudge against the captain. Nevertheless, no such feelings will materialize while they are desperately scrambling to find a lifeboat. When you are using all your emotional energy for the now, it doesn't leave any room for blame and resentment from the past.

People who are complaining about the iceberg won't find a lifeboat. And people looking for the lifeboat are not complaining about the captain.

When you are consumed with making the present the best it can be, past resentments are squeezed out by themselves.

It's an amazingly simple concept to prove.

Imagine you are sitting down, mulling over a resentment from your past—a promotion that went to someone less qualified, the disloyalty of a close friend, maybe an illness.

Now imagine the building you are in begins to shake and

things start flying off the walls. People begin screaming, "Earthquake!"

Where is your resentment now?

It disappeared because the present pushed it out. Resentment of past issues uses the same energy as the crisis in the present. If you are using that energy for today, there will be none left for yesterday.

Thus the only thing we can do with the past is to learn from it, and anything other than that is not only counter-productive, it's worse—it's self-destructive.

In a similar fashion, the only thing we can do with the present is to have fun with it.

When a person synonymously views "busy" with "fun," then life can really start moving.

And this is how winners operate. They have fun with what they are doing today.

But fun doesn't necessarily mean what most people mean by fun.

If you had the privilege of being in one of the landing boats at the invasion of Europe in World War II, you almost cer-

Landing boat at Normandy Beach, WWII. (Courtesy of Shutterstock.)

tainly were not singing, "Happy days are here again." Given the choice, Miami Beach would be your destination, not Normandy Beach.

Twenty years later however, I doubt you could find a single soldier who would not declare that moment as the highlight of their lives.

This is not as uncommon as you might think. I have yet to meet a woman who did not cherish her childbirth experience, even after a multi-day labor.

Whenever we've had a major obstacle to overcome, we invariably look back at that period and realize we were having an incredibly engaging and fulfilling experience. Whether it was the early years of raising children, or a struggling business, adolescence, or school, hindsight brightens every challenge.

[A note from my editor: "Rabbi, reading your point reminds me of what I consider my most heroic act—pushing through a hospital surgery door and pulling my five-year-old son off the operating table. I sensed it was an unnecessary surgery, and was correct! I've often wished I could summon up that courage at will. It was traumatic at the time, but I felt great about myself and look back at my action in wonder.]

Exactly!

The more problems we have had, and the more insurmountable they seemed to be at the time, then the more we look back and reminisce.

That is what I mean by fun.

Everyone does this, but winners do it better. Not only do they enjoy it, they realize they are enjoying it as they are going through it.

It's not just how highly successful people live, it's the only way to live if you want to win.

Why?

Unless we think of it as fun, then we are simply not going to take it on.

If the challenge or obstacle isn't fun, then by default we will avoid it. As such, when we associate busy with pain, then we will do our best to avoid the challenges (read: opportunities) that will bring great success.

When Steve Jobs went back into Apple it wasn't because he needed the money. Far from it. It was because he saw that reviving a now floundering company was going to be this kind of fun. When Meg Whitman took over Hewlett-Packard, it wasn't because she needed money, she did very well as the CEO of Ebay. It was because she saw that saving HP from almost certain demise was going to be fun.

We can think about this another way too.

Unless you are a minimum wage worker in China, you are more than likely being paid to solve problems that machines cannot.

Today, anything that is mindless is being outsourced.

Your most valuable earning tool is your brain.

The more your job needs your brain (as opposed to brawn), then invariably the more you are being paid. Brawn is measured in weight and horsepower, while brain-power is measured in stress. If your work is stressful, it means you are needed. When you appreciate this, your frustration at work will dissipate.

I was counseling a very successful businessman who was bemoaning the pressures of running his multi-million dollar business. After explaining his company to me, I asked why he had no competition, and he told me it was very difficult to produce what he manufactures. I then pointed out that his stress was there because he was in business—if his work wasn't so aggravating, then he would be out of work because so many other companies would be able to do what he did.

A few days later he told me how much his attitude had changed. Now he goes into work and has a great time. Every problem that comes across his desk is a guarantee of his and his company's security.

When you view your daily stress as the reason you have a job, it changes the way you look at stress. Invariably, the people with the most stressful jobs have the highest job security.

Stress is the cost of entry, and therefore also the barrier, to competition. Instead of bemoaning your stress, try this, it's amazingly therapeutic: Be grateful you have it.

CHAPTER 9
The Present Mess

This is how winners think.

They wake up in the morning and they see what we all see, a mess.

The difference is they don't expect anything less, while everyone else does.

Today is, and always is, a mess.

And what is more, fixing that mess will be fun!

The mistake most people make is that they go to bed wishing that when they wake up there won't be a mess.

This simple mistake is an absolute disaster. And people who do it take what would otherwise be a great day, and ruin it.

Let me explain.

Einstein saw the laws of physics, as they were stated at the time, as a mess.

The various and insufficient theories of physics that had been built up over the previous centuries was a maze. After struggling to unravel that tangle he ultimately formulated E=MC2, or the Theory of Relativity.

What did everyone else do with that mess of physics? Surely they saw the same problems that Einstein saw? Yes, but they simply accepted it.

Einstein became Einstein because he decided to clean up the mess.

Whether articulated or not, our goal, when we wake up in the morning, is to end the day in the same spot as we woke up.

Physically and mentally.

We intend to put our head on a pillow with the same peace of mind, equilibrium, and tranquility as when we lifted our head off that very same pillow.

Maybe even better.

And when we wake up we expect to be met with all that tranquility intact.

However, not soon after we open one of our eyes then the chaos starts, and it doesn't let up.

No matter how prepared we are, every day is unpredictable. Sometimes a disaster comes from work. Other times, you walk into the office and all is fine, then you get a call from your child's school.

A mess or disaster is always lurking around the corner and coming out in the most unexpected ways.

No matter how tranquil you manage to feel at the end of the day, lurking in the eaves are the forces of existence whose job it is to ruin what you have accomplished.

One would think (mistakenly) that the world should stay where we left it. That whatever level of transcendence we achieve, the next day should begin where we left off.

But it's as though the world needs our presence to keep it in place, and when we leave, it all starts to fall apart. We live in a kind of bowling alley of existence. But in this game, we set the pins up and the machine at the end of the lane knocks them down. That machine is called life. No matter how many pins we set up, when we return the next day, they are all lying on the ground again.

And our job is to pick them all up, again!

Now, consider this.

In bowling it's called fun. In video games it's called fun. In golf it's called fun. But in life it's (mistakenly) called aggravation.

It only feels like aggravation because we were hoping today would be a breeze; that we would wake up and hear violins playing, doves chirping, and find a hot breakfast waiting for us. Everyone would be singing our praises and Warren Buffet decided to make us his heir.

Hoping that will happen is what I call future thinking.

Why future?

Life is like those marines landing on Normandy Beach. They are there because they have some vague idea about a brave new world of the future. But right now bullets are flying, missiles are exploding, and people are dying—it's brutal.

Our lives are somewhat like that. We need a dream of the future, but the path to get there is brutal.

The future is for dreaming, and today is for making things happen. Which means fixing the mess.

Don't think about today the way you should be thinking about tomorrow. I am in no way suggesting we stop wishful thinking. What I am suggesting, is that kind of thinking is for the future. Right now, right here, needs reality thinking, that will get you to the dream you want. However, if you put wishful thinking in the present, you end up with a boat load of disappointment.

Let's take this a little deeper.

We are built in such a way that, when we apply the wrong thinking to our day, we get a shot of pain—it's like putting our hand on a hot burner, or our finger in an electric socket. That pain is telling us: This is not good for you, don't do this, don't think this way.

It's when we want the present to be smooth and calm that we get the pain stimuli, because it's not helpful to think like that.

Every type of pain we have has a different name because it has a different purpose. The specific pain we are focusing on now is commonly known as aggravation.

It's all according to degree, but the more we think the present should be easy, then the more we are going to be aggravated. If we go to sleep having solved the day's mess, and expect it to stay that way when we wake up, then we are going to be sorely aggravated.

Listen, no news outlet ever went out of business because there was a lack of news. There is always a catastrophe to report. Life is built in such a way that disasters are a constant. The news is counting on it, every day, everywhere.

Only the future is peaceful.

Let's use some examples to understand this idea more fully.

No one says to their spouse as they go to play a game of basketball or golf: "Honey, I'm just going out with the guys to get frustrated."

When we view these kinds of challenges as fun, then we have fun. And when we don't, like at work, then fun is not what we experience.

When we view a challenging and frustrating game of golf or tennis as fun, it therefore is fun. But when a person expects their day at work to be tranquil, it will, by necessity, be frustrating and not fun.

The opposite is also true. Plan a day of fishing and the challenges are easily tolerated. Because that's what fishing is! But if you head off and expect the fish to chase you down and jump into the boat, then you are surely going to be complaining as you wait for a nibble at the end of your line.

Life is no less challenging.

Fix in your mind that today is going to be exciting, and nothing will stop you from enjoying it.

I find this fascinating. The Hebrew word for day (yom) is built from the same Hebrew word for sea (yam). The meaning for me is this: The very nature of water is unpredictability. And a day is just the same.

For many people a day sailing on the water is fun because it's unpredictable. A day on the sea is fun because you don't know what you will get. That is the same way to think about your day.

It's impossible to have fun with the predictable.

Yes, we do enjoy having the things we like the way we like them. But the thrills of life don't come from doing what we like, it comes from doing things that are unpredictable.

If you make the mistake of scripting your life in such a way that it excludes the unpredictable, it will suck the fun and joy out too.

I have a student who volunteered to join the army, however he was disappointed when they wouldn't let him become a paratrooper. Personally, if I were thrown out of a United Airlines plane from 30,000 feet on my way to Atlanta, I would be somewhat perturbed—but for him, it would make his day (as long as he had a parachute).

When you view your work like being in the Olympics, you will wake up ready for the adventure. And, most importantly, you will have a great time in the process.

The absolute truth is this: Not only can the challenges of today be fun—we can't live without them.

In the tumultuous early years of Apple, Steve Jobs was stripped of all responsibility and given an office (and nothing more). He wasn't fired, just reduced to staring at a wall. He had no authority, nor any responsibility. Basically, they didn't want to fire him, but equally, they didn't want him running Apple in any fashion.

Now, take your average hippopotamus and give it three meals a day and a cool lake to float in, and it will stay there its entire life. Even two meals. However, just making money and shuffling papers on a desk was torture for Jobs. He couldn't do it.

And neither could you!

Human beings can tolerate any challenge that is thrown their way. Except one: Having no challenge.

Human beings are not happy just being.

People need to overcome adversity. It is so necessary that if we don't have enough adversity, we create it artificially.

It's called Angry Birds, Candy Crush, or Sudoku.

Animals don't try to make their lives more difficult than they already are. Lions are not going for the fittest gazelles. No lion ever said to the rest of the pack "Forget the weak ones. It's too easy and embarrassing. We need a challenge."

The reason is because they don't need to overcome anything to achieve tranquility.

Even if you could give your children a zoo-like dream world void of any difficulty, they will inevitably mess it up, because they need strife.

As every billionaire will testify, giving your children all they need so they never need to work is not good for anyone—especially the children.

"There's nothing people like me worry about more, how ... do we keep our money from destroying our kids?"
—Curtis L. Carlson
Owner of the Radisson Hotel chain

If you don't believe me, read the newspaper reports of what the children of the very rich do with their lives; it's far from tranquil, or even pretty.

"If you don't watch out, you can set up a situation where a child never has the pleasure of bringing home a paycheck."
—T. Boone Pickens Jr.

Why can't the children of the super-rich just sit in a deck chair all day long and sip on piña colada's? Why do they engage in dangerous and even illegal endeavors which often ruin the tranquil lives their parents gifted them?

Because they know this simple and absolute truth: Tranquility without adversity is more painful than any adversity you and I are going through right now.

This truth is very hard for most people to acknowledge. Especially those stuck in adversity. They so much want to believe that when it is all over they will be happy. It's hard to appreciate that having no adversity is worse.

But it is.

This is why institutions that lock people up with very little to challenge them, whether that's a prison or a psychiatric hospital, struggle to help their charges. Making their lives easier is not easier.

We need a challenge to thrive, but at the same time we hate it when it arrives.

Isn't it odd, we can enjoy watching an action movie, but when a similar drama unfolds in our own lives we fall apart?

If we had a day like James Bond we would surely complain. Yet, when we watch it on the big screen, it seems appealing.

It seems appealing because we all want a life filled with challenge. And, in truth, we do have such a life. Our challenges are really our fun—and they're just as exciting.

A video game is not exciting if it's erasing dots on a screen, but it is when it's fighting gangsters on the streets of New York. The more real it feels, the more fun it is.

Real is fun.

Today is real.

In sum, today is made for us to have fun. All you have to do is wake up and look in your Inbox.

We just don't appreciate it until someone makes a movie about it. Looking back at the Moon Shot, or the Cuban Missile Crisis, or D-Day, or any number of very challenging moments, it's easy to long to live a life like that.

That is, unless you really do have a life like that.

But at some future date we will look back and miss the times (and their problems) we are living in now.

I am not proposing that you should seek adventure for its own sake, mostly because you don't have to.

Your life is already a drama. And your alarm clock in the morning is the director's call for "Lights, camera, action." Enjoy today. You're in a movie!

The now is the fun. In the future we will be able to see how exciting this really was; the trick is to enjoy it now.

The choice happens when we wake up. When we find today's mess, we can either panic and wish it would go away, or realize this is my day of excitement.

And when we see it as exciting, it really is a thrill.

"But what is work and what is not work? Is it work to dig, to carpenter, to plant trees, to fell trees, to ride, to fish, to hunt, to feed chickens, to play the piano, to take photographs, to build a house, to cook, to sew, to trim hats, to mend motor bicycles? All of these things are work to somebody, and all of them are play to somebody. There are in fact very few activities which cannot be classed either as work or play according as you choose to regard them."
—George Orwell
from *The Road to Wigan Pier*

Golf is quite pointless. It's much easier to just pick up the golf ball and place it in the hole. The fun is in the challenge. However, the person who is paid to find the leftover golf balls and put them in a bucket is not enjoying it like the person playing the game.

Your day is no less challenging than a game of golf. Thus, if you can enjoy golf, why can't you enjoy your day?

The mistake people make is that whatever job or life they have, the harder it becomes the worse they think of it.

Unless of course, it's golf or Angry Birds!

What happens in a game of computer space invaders when you destroy all the aliens?

You go up a round. What happens in the next round? Exactly the same as the previous one, but this time there are more aliens, they have more armaments, and they are coming in even faster. And shockingly this keeps happening with each successive round.

But that's not how we want it to go in life. If video games were designed the way we think life should go, then each successive round would get progressively easier. The final round would allow you to defeat the evil invaders with a tap on any key!

If you belong to a golf course that is not particularly challenging, you will look for a more difficult one. Yet when it comes to life, we want all the greens to slope downward so the balls roll effortlessly into the appropriate holes!

Whatever our goal happens to be we tend to think of the obstacles to our success as impediments to the fun. As such, most people think problems are actually stopping them from having fun. They mistakenly believe that if, and when, they have no problems, they will really enjoy life. But golf, and every other sport, proves otherwise. If we can view golf this way, then surely our lives, which are far more consequential and real, can and should also be fun.

Why?

Because it's more fun if you are playing for real.

If you make minimum wage, then gambling is fun at 25 cents a hand. But if you are worth $15 billion, even though it's the exact same game it is no fun unless each hand is $100,000 or more. In other words: The more consequential, the more fun.

Let me explain this another way.

A fish is made to swim, a bird is made to fly. It's very possible to keep a bird in a cage for ten years and then one day open that cage and it will not fly away. It has forgotten what it is.

A bird is made to fly and a human being is made to solve problems. That is why we surround ourselves with all kinds of problems. We watch the news about problems, we read about problems. If there aren't enough problems on CNN we pick up a disaster novel.

We are so intensely built to solve problems that it makes us very uncomfortable living with an unsolved one. Pose a riddle and you can entertain people for long periods, even though the solution to the riddle will bear no fruit. Just the idea of leaving something unfinished or unanswered makes people very uncomfortable.

Put an almost finished jigsaw or crossword puzzle in front of a group of friends and it will be hard for them to leave it alone.

Puzzles are magnets. We are simply drawn toward solving mysteries.

The global market for games is staggering, $66 billion just in computer games alone (source: Newzoo 2013). When we consider that games add nothing tangible to the quality of our lives, it's a remarkable expenditure. It's not like food, clothing, or shelter.

So what need do these games fill?

A very basic one.

We are built for solving problems. And the perfect problem that we are exquisitely designed and purposed to solve is called "today."

Today is a mess. That's the problem. Your mission, and your game, is to untangle and solve that mess.

Every single day.

Sound like fun?

Yes, if you think of it like chess or golf.

Today is a mess and every today will be a mess, and that is why it and you are here.

This is the stark truth: Those problems in your life are not the cause of your misery. They are the essence of your happiness.

If you didn't have problems, you would be truly miserable.

Nothing gets us so engaged as real life disasters in the making, and nothing makes us feel more fulfilled than when we devise a solution.

George Burns famously quipped, "How come all the people who know how to run the country are cutting hair or driving a cab?"

It's true, we can't help but opine about what the government should do, even though they aren't asking for our advice. We can't help but solve problems even though it makes no difference.

If you have a job then you are paid to solve problems, and if you don't have a job, then your problem is trying to find one.

We define ourselves according to the type and degree of the problems we solve. Accountants solve financial problems; social workers solve relationship problems; vets, animal problems; parents, kid problems.

We and life are made for each other. Your days are meant to be a mess, and you are meant to fix that mess. Believing that you are going to wake up floating in some kind of equilibrium goo of bliss is an act of delusion. Unfortunately, most people suffer from it!

If your life experience tells you anything, it is that you are going to wake up to some kind of mess (yet to be defined) and you are going to be challenged to fix it.

The degree of the challenge is the degree to which you can enjoy life. And if you deny the problem and push it away, then you will, of necessity, seek to fill the void with an artificial crisis—which can be anything from the latest video game or 3D drama.

Unfortunately, though, no matter how many pixels it has, it's never real enough to have real fun.

Tell yourself when you wake up in the morning: "I am going to have to deal with the mess anyway, so I might as well have fun." And you will!

Not fun while you are doing it, but fun in doing it.

Rise to the occasion and you will see for yourself how easy it is to enjoy the day!

What is more, when you do this, you will immediately begin to lose the negative emotions connected with the past. It's like a bonus life gives you for enjoying life.

Advisory Warning:

In sum, whenever you feel the emotions of blame, resentment, or even guilt invading your consciousness, instead of tackling them head on, realize they are only able to rise up because you are missing out on the opportunity called "Today."

This is going to be a lot easier on your second reading of the book, after you understand all three days and how they all fit together.

Photo: Handicapped Athlete.
Courtesy of Shutterstock

CHAPTER 10
The Worst Word in the English Language

You get more business from the business you lose, than the business you win.

Understanding The Past

Soon after Meg Whitman became Hewlett-Packard's CEO they lost a $350 million Microsoft order that went to rival Dell. That in itself was bad enough, but this was HP's fifth such beating in a row.

This time however, Whitman called Microsoft's CEO Steve Ballmer and asked for a report on what they did wrong.

Microsoft obliged and listed nine ways that HP blew it, price not being the only issue.

Using that report as her blueprint, she set out on turning HP around.

Vindication came within a year when they vied with Dell on another bid. This time HP won the order, $530 million worth of servers. (Source: *Forbes* May 2013)

Your Past Knows the Truth

There are two things you need to know about your past.

First, and most importantly, it is not possible for it to contain anything that precludes you from winning. You cannot possibly mess up enough to stop you from winning.

It doesn't matter what you did in your past, it just can't be that bad.

That doesn't mean there aren't people who do tragically ruin their lives, it's just that you cannot be one of them.

Why?

You wouldn't be reading this book if you were. People in that much denial don't read books like this.

The second truth you need to know is that your past is not holding you back. In fact, it's quite the opposite. Your past is driving you forward. It is the force that is actually pushing you to read this book.

It is precisely because you are so fed up with your own performance that you are venturing out of your comfort zone to see if there is anything out there that can help.

The power of the past is that it contains incredible determination.

Your resolve, grit, and perseverance are derived from your past.

No one can preach the evils of nicotine like a recovering smoker. No one is more an evangelist for sobriety than a recovering alcoholic. And no one is going to expound on the value of education like a fifty-year-old learning how to read.

It's the past that creates a powerful present. That kind of resolve and success is waiting for you—all you have to do is look in your past.

It's that powerful.

In fact, the past has so much power that it makes people very afraid of it.

As such, the past is like acid; you either use it properly or it becomes corrosive.

The only thing you can't do with the past is bury it.

There is simply no such thing as ignoring it. When you try to deny your past, all you are really doing is not talking about it, but that doesn't stop the acid from slowly leaking out and burning.

Not talking about your past is about as effective as not talking about the iceberg that is about to hit the Titanic. It never works out well.

But the real tragedy of denial is that the past is nowhere near as bad as you imagine it to be. In fact, your past will bring you phenomenal success.

When a car is totaled, it doesn't necessarily mean it's completely decimated or even immobile; it simply means the cost of fixing it is greater than the remaining value.

You can total a car, you can total a house, but you can't total a life.

Mistakes are never more damaging than the value of the lessons that can be derived from them.

And that's the purpose of the past. To learn from it.

If yesterday was bad, figure out how not to repeat it. Because success is going to come from knowing why you lost.

HP's mistakes were not worse than the value of the lessons. Said another way: The lessons learned easily made up for any mistakes.

This is true for all of us!

"Problems are good."
—Meg Whitman
CEO of Hewlett-Packard and former CEO of eBay

Please pay attention to this next point because it is key to great success.

Failure occurs because your understanding of how business works, relationships work, or life in general work, were incomplete. Your understanding got you so far, but at a certain point, it could not get you any further.

Look at our example with HP. They consistently failed because they misunderstood how to do business, at least at that level. But when they used their past to learn, then great success awaited them.

Are there things in your life where you are consistently failing? Learn from Whitman's example. Success is also waiting for you!

The reason Orville and Wilbur's first airplane did not get very far is because it was built on the principles of aerodynamics known at the time.

Most of the competition gave up at that point. But the Wright brothers asked a different question. They asked our question: How do we learn from the past?

When we learn from the past, we open the doors to great success. Orville and Wilbur failed on their first attempt because they were working with the same knowledge and playbook as everyone else.

Similarly, just as you have failed, so has everyone else. The person who asks our question is the one who enters the next realm.

That person will possess a much rarer knowledge. When Orville and Wilbur figured it out on December 17, 1903 in Kitty Hawk they owned a knowledge no one else had.

"In the land of the blind, the one-eyed man is king."
—Erasmus of Rotterdam, 16th century

Winners know things other people don't.

That knowledge is the ultimate advantage, and it's found in failure. That is why winners love problems.

Why is this so? Because it's easier to learn from the bad than the good.

Don't put too much stock in success. The case of HP and Dell is very illustrative here: After five straight wins it would have been challenging at best for Dell (not Hewlett-Packard) to learn anything that would prevent their upcoming loss.

"Having no problems was the biggest problem of all."
—Taiichi Ohno, VP of production at Toyota

Not so when Dell finally did lose. At that point, learning was relatively easy.

Success comes through failure. By studying failure that is.

And if there is one thing your business and life has plenty of, it is failure. No one gets it right the first time around, or consistently.

There are only two types of problems in life, the ones you know about and the other kind.

If you don't think you have problems, then look harder.

There is always plenty to learn from, and if you do, ultimate success is certain. Why?

If you consistently learn from your mistakes, you will inevitably get it right. Eventually.

This is what winners do.

It sounds so incredibly obvious and simple. The problem is most people don't do it.

We all do things we regret; it's the nature of living. You simply cannot script life.

"There is no one so righteous who does good without making mistakes."
—King Solomon, Ecclesiastes 7:20

What divides all of humanity is what happens after the mistake. No matter what advantage you might have, what you do after things go wrong is going to determine the quality of your life going forward.

It is when we try to forget and deny that we build dysfunction into our businesses and lives. You can erase a computer code, you can even erase a page from a history book, but you can't erase your own mistakes. That's because the thinking that made the mistake has not changed. And therefore, it will just be repeated.

Thus denial and blame are completely counterproductive activities—whether it's blaming someone else, or even ourselves.

What is blame?

Blame is wishing the past would be different. Which is the same as denial, except with denial it's ignoring the past. With blame it's ignoring your role in that past.

Blame is debilitating because you want to change what has happened, but obviously can't.

When you blame, you are caught in an emotional vice that has no relief. You desperately want a result different from the one you have. You also think it's someone else's fault.

That does not happen if you are willing to learn from what went wrong. What we should do is learn from the past. To do that, you have to accept that the past cannot be changed.

It sounds simple.

So why can't people do it?

A person plagued with blame simply can't turn off the switch, because doing so would mean they'd have to give up their anger and frustration and accept what has been.

I have had this experience multiple times. I'm waiting in the airport departure lounge for a plane that's already significantly late. Then an official reluctantly announces the flight has been cancelled. Instantaneously two groups begin to form.

The first group is angry and starts blaming whomever they can find. The other group starts looking for an alternative to getting home.

By the time the first group realizes there is no hope of flying out their other options have been taken by the second group.

Blame is wishing what was, wasn't. While you are busy blaming your staff, blaming the general public, blaming even your family, the government, or even blaming the United Nations, the successful people of life have already taken their company public!

I know that sounds ridiculous, but it's really what you are doing when you say "If only . . ."

"If only x, y, or z had not happened, then my life would not have been ruined," is just another way of placing blame.

BLAME (and its synonyms) IS THE WORST WORD IN THE ENGLISH LANGUAGE.

Take a moment now and ask yourself: What things have happened to you that you are blaming for your lack of success? What about today? Did anything happen recently that you felt made your life more difficult?

It doesn't have to be catastrophic. It just made your commute longer, or lunch less pleasant. A parking ticket, traffic accident, neighbor, friend, and let's not forget your spouse. Did anything or anyone make your life even a little bit more difficult?

If you answered "yes," welcome to the world of blame!

Now here is the truth, none of those things are holding you back—it's only your blame of those things that is stopping you.

After the disastrous news of the Titanic hit the world, two things happened. Some people went looking for someone to blame, while others wanted to learn how to build a safer boat. Both the British and American governments set up inquiries, and while the British primarily blamed the iceberg (and only tangentially the ship's officers), their American counterpart listed key failings that resulted in new maritime safety legislation that is still in effect today.

Blame is not unjustified. It's just pointless. It's always the person who wants to learn that creates a better and safer world. For themselves and others.

Blame clouds responsibility and precludes the possibility of improvement.

I am not saying that negligence should be ignored; it's just that punishing it should come from the desire to build a safer boat. On the other hand, blame pushes people to exact a punishment far beyond whatever the negligence deserves.

You can't say "if only" about a mistake and also want to learn from it.

"If only" really means: "I wish it had been different."

Thinking life "should" have been different will inevitably cause blame. When you blame, you are not learning from the past, you are really engaged in the emotional equivalent of trying to change that past. Your emotional brain is engaged in the past, the way you should be engaged with the present, that is, by trying to change it.

Change

We have an inner drive to change things, but there is a real limit to what that drive can be applied to. Intellectually we know we can only change the present, but emotionally we don't understand why we can't change the past.

That is because emotions don't understand time. Our emotions "think" the past and the present are the same. So if we can change the present, why not the past?

If you grew up in a home where your parents walked around constantly fretting over past grievances, then almost certainly you are going to be afflicted with the same habit of trying to change the past.

Change is for the present, exclusively.

Blame and regret are the emotions you experience when

you think about yesterday the way you should be thinking about today.

What is fascinating is that when you apply the way of thinking that we call "blame" to the present, it's not blame anymore; it's a completely different experience, one that is energizing and productive, one that really helps you with life.

The story is told of a traveler waiting for his flight. He is told that due to overbooking he is being bumped from the plane.

By the time he gets home, his righteous indignation mixed with pure frustration gets him through the usual corporate barriers—until he is speaking directly with the CEO of the airline. After spending a good ten minutes raging through a vitriolic and scathing criticism, the CEO calmly asks if he could respond.

Our #1 complainer in a fit of false humility, agrees to this request.

The CEO softly responds, "As much as I sympathize with your frustration, I am sure you will agree with me that your suffering cannot compare to the experiences of the other passengers and their families who were on that plane."

"Why is that?" the man sheepishly responds.

"Because, I am sorry to have to tell you, that plane crashed."

Now, where did that man's blame go?

That blame has now become praise and gratitude for the airline employees.

In all likelihood, he might even refuse a refund.

But we don't have to be so dramatic: If instead of bumping him, the airline had told him there was another flight at the other end of the airport waiting for him, his energies would transfer to making that departure.

It's blame when it's something that has already happened, but when the experience is in the present then the blame is transformed into something effective. It becomes helpful and sometimes even pleasant.

Change is good, but not when you're trying to change the past. Then it becomes destructive. Our traveler can't change the fact that he has been bumped. That is the past. Trying to rewrite what happened will only lead to anger and frustration. Change is good, and only good, in the present.

When you try and change the past, what you are doing is thinking about yesterday the way you should be thinking about today.

It's using "Today" thinking for yesterday.

Today is for making a difference, as opposed to yesterday, which is for learning.

The opportunity to alter the outcome is only in the present. Today is all about figuring out how to end up with a different outcome than the one you'll get if you do not engage in any meaningful activity.

Someone ripped you off yesterday. Or maybe you paid too much for gas last week. Your partner embezzled company funds and you went bankrupt three years ago. Or you tore up the winning lottery ticket by mistake. The list of past regrets is as long as there are days in history.

It's emotionally enticing to berate the past and its perpetrators. It feels good and it feels like you are accomplishing something. But while you are spending two to three hours venting, J.K. Rowling is writing another book.

Blame is not for winners—it's for whiners.

Whether it's the fault of others or self-inflicted, stressing over other people's malicious activity (blame) or your stupidity (guilt) is not an act of learning from the past. It's trying to change something that cannot be changed. It has already happened!

I don't really need to give examples, but these are two blaring blamers that are all too familiar.

Divorcees: People who have gone through a bitter divorce find it even more impossible than most people to learn from their experience.

Disgruntled ex-employees: If you know anyone who has been fired in a way that they view as unjustified, you can forget about trying to point out what they could learn from the pink slip.

This is a tremendous shame, because if they did learn (both in divorce and sacking), they would go on to have great relationships and be phenomenal employees. But they can't because they are caught in the blame game.

A student called me a while ago and asked for a private session. He was upset that he got a bad review from his boss. "Don't they realize how much I give to this company!" he told me.

He was looking for sympathy, but I was more interested in being his friend. And sympathy was not going to help him.

I suggested the following: Instead of berating your employer, try to figure out how they might be right.

If you want to win you have to find where you are wrong. And learn from it.

I am happy to say that even though at first he was not too pleased, he eventually got it. And, not surprisingly, he achieved greater success at work.

Here is an extreme example of futility: A man takes a $1,000 bill and uses it to light a cigar.

Can anything worthwhile come from such idiocy?

We all understand the parable that nothing good comes from destroying money. It's also true with time. Nothing good comes from wasting it. We are wasting time when we try and change yesterday instead of learning from it.

We aren't using reason when we think we can change yesterday. This is not rational and no one would admit to doing it. We think it emotionally. Who can deny their frustration (emotional thinking) over previously made bad choices?

How many times have you taken a train that got delayed and fretted (and blamed yourself) over the thought you should have taken an alternate form of transportation? Similarly, you bought a plane ticket for a long-planned trip and the following week you saw the same flight for half the cost. How much time would you spend wishing you had waited a few more days?

Soon after we were married, my wife and I visited my family in London where we decided to buy some china with wedding money for our intended home in Los Angeles.

After some very exhaustive shopping, we settled on some stylish but classic dishes made by a small division of Wedgewood that seemed like a great value.

We didn't ship the boxes, as money was very tight for us newlyweds, so we brought it on the plane—air travel was very different in those days. But it was a sorely arduous journey carrying all that china.

That first Thanksgiving in L.A. was a big downer. The biggest retail store in those days featured a full double page ad in the *L.A. Times* with its door buster sale—our china!

Cheaper than we paid for it in England, where it was made.

It took me a while to realize that "if only" thinking doesn't get you anywhere.

Our emotions tell us that if we agonize over the past enough by examining it with excruciating detail, then we can actually change it. It's here that our intellect must instruct our emotions that the past is off limits.

I have been doing marriage counseling for nearly thirty years, and it is very common in infidelity cases for the aggrieved spouse to want detail after detail. They drill their spouse for minutiae that ultimately will solve nothing and bring no reprieve.

As much as I sympathize with the injured spouse, it is nevertheless a bottomless pit because what they really want is to change the past. Their emotions are telling them that if they get enough details, then they can change what happened. This is perfectly understandable, since their emotions are so badly suffering, and it is these same emotions that are looking for reprieve. And because emotions don't distinguish between the present and the past, they go looking in the past for salvation.

We have demons in our head, scars from friends and family who have burnt us and about which we are still bitter. That bitterness comes from this type of thinking. Nothing of course will change or improve until a different question is asked.

How do we learn from the past?

If you find yourself continuously fretting over history, it's because you emotionally believe you can change that history. This is not a victimless sport. You are the victim. You are wasting energy that should be used to change the present. And since you have a limited amount of that energy, once you have emptied it out venting about the past, there is nothing left to improve today.

This is not dissimilar from a grieving relative screaming

expletives at a grave, annoyed at all the abuse the deceased caused them in some fit of hope that the person lying six feet down is getting all of this and can do something about it. Tormenting yourself does not change what has already happened. Emotions do not open a portal in time.

If we took the emotional energy used in these pointless efforts and used them instead for the present, we would see a tremendous increase in effectiveness. I have lost count of how many people waste a good hour or more seeking my counsel, only to spend it complaining about some past abuse without the slightest mention of their plans, goals, and future. How much more effective they could be if all that anger was channeled toward unlocking the opportunities in front of them!

What would it look like if instead of trying to change the past, we used that energy to change the present?

It would look like a winner.

A machine performs its actions according to the commands in its software. Any fault in the program is going to be reflected in the actions it takes. As such, when we don't learn from history (i.e., our mistakes), then our software doesn't change and we keep repeating those same mistakes, again and again. This is why denial of our errors is so ineffective and self-destructive.

However, truly learning from a mistake will invariably involve recognizing our own faults in the process. After all, it's an error in our programing that made the problem. Once we recognize the error in the code, we will be able to rewrite our very own software.

Blaming others is pointless since we can only change our own software. And you can't change that until you learn. This means wanting to learn from the past in the same way a computer programmer wants to find the fault in the code.

Jeff Bezos, the founder and CEO of Amazon.com, describes how a major glitch in their early software allowed customers to bill Amazon.

To say the least, it was inappropriate for the customer to do such a thing. Bezos could have spent the time tracking down every last dollar, but he didn't blame the customers. Blame and resentment is not how winners think—they learn from the past. And in this case, by rewriting the software.

It's your software that allowed the mistakes in your life to happen.

Isn't this obvious? If we learned from the past we would change the present and so make fewer mistakes, which in turn would give us less to regret in the future. If we don't learn, then we can look forward to more of the same kind of resentment.

Would you keep using a calculator that you knew was giving you the wrong numbers? Put gasoline in your car that you knew ruined the engine, or buy an umbrella that you knew did not keep you dry? In every other area it is easy to see how important it is to learn from the past, why is this not so easy with our own mistakes?

Because people really believe they can change the past.

How do you know if you are one of those people?

Here is a simple litmus test: The telltale sign that a person believes they can change the past is blame, guilt, or resentment.

When we think about the past the way we should be thinking about the present, that is attempting to change it, then we end up in a quagmire of blame or guilt.

Take again our computer example—a glitch in the software

is going to produce a warning message on the screen. We are that computer, and the warning message is blame, resentment, and guilt.

I am sure you know more than a few friends and family who are stuck in the past. They can't get anything done because they simply stress over the resentments they are bearing from their history.

Please be aware, I am not denying that people may have truly abused you. But what I am saying is that the abuse will continue as long as you are stuck resenting it.

The best way to punish an abuser is to learn from what they did to you and improve your life.

As we mentioned in Chapter Five, Louis Zamperini, the World War II hero, met his former tormentors after the war. In that encounter, who admired who?

I am 100 percent certain his captors looked at him with awe and admiration. He did something they had not done, and maybe could never do—learn from the past.

Zamperini went looking for them, when really it was the captors who should have been looking for Zamperini. But they didn't look, because they were not trying to learn from what happened. Rarely do abusers learn.

Think of the human body as an ultimate machine that has a built in warning system that shoots pain whenever it approaches danger, especially self-destruction. That is exactly what happens when we use the past in these unproductive ways, we get a painful shot called blame or resentment. It's our own self-defense mechanism sending a warning signal for us to STOP.

It's very similar to a warning siren on a highly sophisticated nuclear submarine when a crewmember is about to do something potentially fatal.

Guilt is an utterly pointless and painful emotion. This alone should be enough to tell us we should not be thinking in ways that produce this feeling.

I can guess what you are thinking: "Easier said than done." Feelings of blame are stubborn thorns not easily budged.

However, each particular day and its associated thinking is a piece of a total puzzle.

The past has one puzzle shape, the present another, and the future a third. The thinking that goes along with that particular day is the picture on the puzzle piece.

When you understand the whole picture, everything will fit together. As such, trying to change one part by itself is more difficult than need be.

Also, once you use the right thinking for any one of the three time frames (past, present, and future) then it will nudge the other days into their correct placement too. In other words, when we get one of the days right, we force the other two into the correct alignment.

For example, when the past is used for learning, then the present will automatically be used for change, and the future for goals and dreams.

It works the same way for the present. When the present is used correctly for change and fun, then the past becomes exclusively a place of learning, and the future similarly falls into place.

This might sound abstract and absurdly simple, but finding simple solutions to the fundamental issues in everyone's life is exactly what this book is all about.

Just like a jigsaw puzzle, figuring out where the first piece goes makes the second piece much easier to find. As such, the first puzzle piece will cause the other days to fall into place. That first piece in the puzzle is future thinking. As we are going to realize, getting the future in order is the easiest of the days. It's the least encumbered with angst, and while it also has its own misunderstandings, it's easier to deal with than past blame or present disappointment.

"It's no use going back to yesterday, because I was a different person then."
—Lewis Carroll
Alice's Adventures in Wonderland

CHAPTER 11
The Big Deal

Charles Lindbergh became a major celebrity for being the first person to fly solo across the Atlantic in 1927. But today, announcing to the world you crossed that same distance would not even earn you an upgrade.

For sure, the obstacles Lindbergh had to overcome were nowhere near as simple as choosing an aisle or window seat. Staying awake for thirty-three hours with no autopilot was just one of the many problems he had to contend with. Nevertheless, some achievements are still momentous even if they are no longer unique.

Literacy is one of them. Because we live in a world where these proficiencies are common, we lose the sense of their great value.

In the ancient world the ability to read and write would give anyone incredible leverage. Even today, literacy gives you a tremendous advantage in a world where approximately one in five people are still illiterate.

But do you know why you can read and write?

It's not because you are so smart—it's because the goal is no big deal.

This is a very interesting and important point, the lack of awe at these and other similar accomplishments allows us to achieve them.

But it is simultaneously the reason we minimize our abilities. A person who learned to read a thousand years ago would have been considered a genius. Yet, it is essentially no less difficult today.

We just don't appreciate how much we have accomplished because everyone is doing it.

I recently met someone who ran the mile in under four minutes, while still in high school! Unfortunately, I can't remember his name, and that is the point. What Roger Bannister accomplished in 1954 has become mundane—like reading and writing.

This is an incredible lesson we need to note. At the time of Bannister, no one (other than he) could run that fast, and therefore no one (other than he) tried. Today it's so common that high school students are doing it. When something is viewed as incredible, as a superhuman type activity, then you need a Bannister or Lindbergh to pull it off. But when it's viewed as the norm, then anyone can try—and many succeed.

The thing stopping you, and anyone, from taking on dreamlike goals is thinking that what you want to do requires a greatness you don't possess.

I have said this same thing to my children before they learned to read: "By this time next year, you will be able to read on your own." However, that goal seemed so daunting to them that they had trouble believing me.

After they learned to read, I pointed out that every goal in life is just as simple. And if you remember this point, that often it is only the dread of the goal that stops us, then the goal itself will not be so challenging. Because of this, many more opportunities will open up for you.

Even though the context for Roosevelt's famous line was completely different, it is still apropos: "The only thing we have to fear is fear itself."

Reminding our children that the fear of goals is unwarranted is an important part of good parenting. Many of us would attempt some mighty spectacular goals if not for this misplaced fear.

When we create an aura of awe or fear around a goal we make it so much harder to achieve. If we lived in a world of near total illiteracy, then most people would view learning to read and write as unrealistic.

As such, so many more things in life are available to us when we minimize their difficulty.

One day you too will look back at what you want to achieve now and realize it was no big deal, just as what you have achieved up to this point that was previously unimaginable to you.

Getting your mind around this idea will make it infinitely easier for you to commit to amazing goals and dreams.

The gap between the illiterate and literate is about the most significant and dramatic divide most people will ever cross. When you appreciate that, you will realize there are few things that are actually out of your reach.

Get yourself in this mindset: What you want to achieve is no big deal, and anything worthwhile is attainable to you.

While growing up in London, whenever I told my father about something I wanted to achieve but felt was way beyond my capacity, his reaction was always the same—he would just look at me with puzzlement. His attitude was not that I was so great, but that the goal was so small, which was a phenomenal motivator and lesson.

One particular event sticks in my mind. While I was in school, I had a part-time sales job in the West End of London. It was Oxford Street, the epicenter of shopping in England, with some of the highest grossing stores in the world. The problem was that I was not such a great salesman, and I only got the job because the manager who hired me was a nice guy and not really cut out for the intense world of high-pressure sales himself. Thus, soon after I was hired, a new manager took over. His name was Mr. Tough. And his hyphenated first name was "No-Nonsense."

Soon after he arrived, he made his presence known with a speech to all the sales people. I don't remember exactly what he said, but it basically went like this. "Next week most of you will be fired." He gave us a target number to reach and if you didn't reach it, you would be out of a job.

I went home very dejected. The target was much higher than any sales I had ever achieved, and only a few people on staff had ever sold that much. The store clearly did not generate enough business, and therefore a large number of us were doomed.

When I told my father I thought I'd need to find another job, he just looked at me with his confused look and simply stated, very matter-of-factly, that this was not impossible, and if it wasn't impossible, then I shouldn't worry about it.

There were two people who were shocked that I got the requisite amount of sales—the new manager and me. After that I became one of his favorites, which I think was more because my success vindicated his technique as a manager than because of my actual accomplishment.

My father was pleased, but not surprised. If you believe people can achieve great things, then you won't be surprised when they achieve them.

The opposite is also true.

When you make the goal no big deal, then it's easy. As a manager myself, I have used this same technique to great effect with my team; it's amazing what you can do when you think of the goal as a piece of cake.

I have been fortunate to meet people who have achieved what most view as astounding. But they don't think of their achievements in that light. They, like my father, really don't think of what they did as any big deal. It's not that they aren't cognizant of everyone else's admiration—they just think it's misplaced. This is not false humility; they really believe this is the way to view it. And it is.

I am certain that if the news would report kids who learned to swim, read, or ride a bicycle in the same tenor as Lindbergh crossing the Atlantic, then the number of people achieving those goals would drop dramatically.

Thus, it's this very attitude—"it's no big deal"—that enables successful people to achieve what everyone else considers grand. In other words: If the common attitude in 1954 was that running a mile in under four minutes was no big deal, then Bannister would have been competing with teenagers who breezed past him!

People who achieve great things think about their endeavors the same way you and I think about reading and writing.

This concept is very different from how we typically try to motivate people, whether a manager pumping up their team or a parent motivating a child. When you try and convince a child they are special, you implicitly set them up for failure. Children soon learn that they are not the only ones being told they have greatness within them. Every other kid in their class has a mom or dad cheering them on. Since it's logically impossible for every kid to be the best, these children soon realize their parents are not objective.

Don't tell your child they are the best; show them that the world is easier than they think. After each accomplishment point out to them that it was not nearly as difficult as they thought it would be. The more they realize that every goal is just as easy, then the more attainable every goal becomes.

It's actually a lot easier to convince your child, or anyone for that matter, that the goal is easy, than it is to convince them that they possess hidden abilities.

The problem is that we have fallen into this notion that only some people possess greatness, and therefore some goals are only available to these greats.

This is just not true. We can all be great, we can all be winners. And, we all win at goals we think are easy, and inevitably fail at ones we think only a superhuman can achieve. It's not the goal that is stopping us, it's how we think about that goal. As Roger Bannister said, "It wasn't a physical boundary, it was a mental one." That's what kept everyone else back.

Winners are not born. Bannister just learned how to think about the goal in a way that made him believe it was possible.

And everyone else didn't. If Bannister had thought about running the four-minute mile the same way as everyone else did, he could not have done it either. It's not talent, or stamina, or strength, or even perseverance. It is far simpler and much more available. He simply realized it was possible.

Winners learn to think about goals in ways that make winning inevitable.

You can learn to think that way too.

"They did not know
it was impossible so they did it"
—Mark Twain

PART 3
CHAPTER 12
The Future

Ambition

Traditional schools are there to educate the motivated, not create the motivation.

Thus, if a student is not achieving their goals, the easiest thing for the school to do is to lower those goals.

A lack of big goals creates low motivation, and typically a school will respond to a student's low motivation by making the goals even smaller.

The problem is that when a child gets frustrated or starts failing, it's a clear sign there is a lack of big motivational goals, not that they need to be in a lower grade.

When my oldest child was involved with sports, she won a trophy if she deserved a trophy. The gap between her and my youngest is sixteen years, but that is even bigger than the number suggests.

During that span a lot changed in the world. Specifically, her younger sibling gets a trophy every season, whether he deserves it or not.

When he first got one, it was a big thrill because he thought he was on par with his elder siblings who have trophies displayed in the room he inherited. But by the third season it became a meaningless experience. He may not be able to articulate why, but what he experienced is that we have lowered the goal to meet the child. As such, it's safe to assume that this is why he's not the athlete his older siblings were.

On June 13, 1935, as a ten to one underdog, Jim Braddock beat Max Baer to become the heavyweight boxing champion of the world.

Ron Howard made a movie about Jim (*Cinderella Man*) because for him to win, Braddock had to overcome something few boxers ever do: He had to come out of retirement and revive his failed career. Boxers rarely, if ever, have comebacks. And if they do, they don't do better the second time around. Boxing is not acting or chess. It's a very, very challenging and brutal sport that has no room for sympathy. You are competing against someone who can only win if you lose. You therefore have to be at your physical peak—and you only get one peak per lifetime.

What pushed Jim back into the ring, driving him to achieve what he couldn't the first time around?

A very, very big goal.

It was the Great Depression. He and his family were living on the edge in a slum apartment. Afraid of losing his children, he did something unheard of, he beat Max Baer. When asked how he did it, Braddock simply said, "I know what I'm fighting for now. Milk."

This is not so strange or rare as we might imagine.

A single mom raising two kids with a fulltime job is going

back into that same ring as Jim Braddock when she takes evening classes to become an accountant—because just like Jim, it's the only way out of poverty.

If this mom can take an accounting course after a full day's work plus an evening with her children's homework, then she obviously could have done the same thing when she was in high school.

What was lacking in her teenage years that caused her to wait until she had two kids, a job, and bills to pay?

Big goals. She wants to send her kids to college.

Don't lower the goal to fit the child. Inspire the child to fit the goal.

But there is also one more thing you need.

Someone who believes in giant goals.

You don't necessarily need someone who believes in your goal, but you need at least one person in your life that believes people can do great things.

We all have seen Star Wars and Harry Potter, but people need real people who believe real people can do great things. Find the people you want to be like, and do your best to be around them. It rubs off.

I am not sure it's impossible, but it's extremely difficult to achieve anything big in a world of small goal people. Being around people who believe in the big is a big help.

My father believes in big goals, not just mine, but his own too. He was always starting something big. I remember vividly his many projects; each time he began one, he was convinced this would be the big one. Of course, he had many failures, but not one of them held him back from trying again.

I can't say he ever spoke of a philosophy of trying; it was

much deeper than that. He lived a philosophy of trying to be great. He wanted to be a great person. Thankfully he has achieved his goal.

"Don't be afraid of death; be afraid of an unlived life."
—Natalie Babbitt
Tuck Everlasting

A Giant Leap
Inspired people don't need steps
and uninspired people won't use them.

When Neil Armstrong crawled out of his Apollo 11 spacecraft to put a dent in the moon, his now famous words, "One small step" were totally appropriate.

The big steps had already been taken down on Earth.

Those were the ones that got him there.

It was relatively easy for President Kennedy to point to the moon, but the team tasked with this incredible feat simply did not know how they were going to pull it off. The obstacles were staggering.

After five landings however, the program was dead. Ironically, what killed off the moon missions, was knowing how to do it!

Inspiration needs ignorance.

If you know all the steps when you start, then it isn't a goal at all, it's a Lego set.

When I was a kid, Lego used to be a great toy. You knew what you wanted to build, and you hoped you had the pieces to do it, you just didn't know how it was all going to fit to-gether—therefore every child had their own Moon Shot.

Today, regrettably, Lego sets come with instructions.

So instead of encouraging a child to find inspiring goals, we are now teaching children to simply follow instructions and rules.

No president today could challenge us to go to the moon, for no other reason than because we know how to do it. Knowing all the steps needed to get to the moon ended the moon missions. The challenge was gone.

From this you can derive an incredible insight: Not knowing how to get there is never the reason people don't try.

Inspired people don't need to know how. And not knowing how is the excuse uninspired people use to give up.

We are not lacking in knowing how to achieve great things, we are only lacking in the great things themselves.

Great goals don't come with instructions; they only come with one thing—the next step.

Every inspirational goal, ever, always had a next.

Without a doubt, when Walt Disney started he had no idea how he was going to build to the happiest place on earth. But he knew that drawing Mickey Mouse was next. Andrew Carnegie had no idea how he was going to become one of the richest people in the world when he landed in America penniless, but he knew that getting to America was the next step.

Winston Churchill most certainly had no idea how he was going to defeat the Nazi's at the beginning of World War II. And when the first shot was fired at Lexington, George Washington could not have possibly predicted that the French, Dutch, and Spanish would join him. Without these allies, he could not have won independence.

But they all knew what had to happen first.

No one who ever achieved anything of value ever knew what the last step would be when they initially set out.

Christopher Columbus certainly had no idea what he would accomplish when leaving port in Spain, but he knew that to do something extraordinary he had to raise the sails.

All any of these people knew was the next step they had to take.

Please note this. When you make a step in the right direction without knowing what you will do after that, then it wasn't a step at all; you just made a giant leap.

An alcoholic has absolutely no idea how he or she is going to conquer their addiction. And even though, to the rest of us it seems just a small step, however for them, walking into that AA meeting is a giant leap.

You don't need to know all the steps to the moon; you just need to know what you need to do tomorrow.

One of the deterrents to winning is thinking you need to know the A-Z to success before you start. If you need to know, and many people do, all the steps to reach the ultimate goal, you will never get there.

Moses had no idea how he would get millions of people to the Promised Land, but he knew what he had to do next: Cross the Red Sea.

The only step you ever need is just the next one. Every great and fantastic goal is equally obscure.

Many people are stuck, trapped in the need to know all the steps.

Finding the next step, just like finding space in a lifeboat, is rare enough. If you need more certainty than that, you probably would have stayed on the Titanic.

We all have our Titanic's. I am sure you have had the experience of trying to untie shoelaces that have become a tangled mess. Or maybe you've been lost in a maze or forest. Maybe disease or daunting financial ruin has zapped all your energy and motivation. In such situations, simply knowing what to do next is all you need.

Not what you need to do after that.

In all of these examples, the best you are usually ever going to know is what's next. And if you can't move until you know the steps after that, then your laces (and your life) are going to stay untied.

Winners have fun not because they win, and not because they succeed, and not because they have money—it's because they know three things:

Where they want to go.

That there will always be a next step.

And those two things are all you need to win.

The last step, the one that completes the mission, is always just as Neil Armstrong described it—the easiest and smallest of them all.

CHAPTER 13
The Past: Learn

Whether it's building a Lego spaceship (before they came with instructions) or the real thing for NASA, every inspiring goal pushes you to the edge of your universe of knowledge.

Beyond that line is the space where winners are made.

If you can learn from others, then for sure do so. It's just that at some point there will be no one to learn from. Those who chart a course ahead will have the advantage. In the dark unknown, you are going to have to figure it out, and at that point, what you understand will be your exclusive knowledge and advantage.

Unfortunately, the vast majority of people, when they venture where no one has gone before, invariably sound the call to retreat back into the safe zone.

It's not easy, and it certainly is not comfortable, but it is absolutely rewarding to the person who ruthlessly learns from their mistakes.

In medicine this technique is sacrosanct. However, in the

rest of life, the reason people struggle to learn from their past is because they haven't envisioned a big enough future—and scientists have.

Can you imagine where we would be if scientists did not venture outside their knowledge limit, or refused to learn from what went wrong?

Penicillin. Alexander Fleming discovered the antibacterial properties of penicillin because a sample of bacteria had accidentally been contaminated with mold.

Rubber Tires. Charles Goodyear discovered vulcanized rubber when a batch of rubber was accidentally left on a stove; he had previously thought that heat was a problem for rubber, not the solution.

Pacemaker. Wilson Greatbatch developed the pacemaker when he accidentally grabbed the wrong resistor from a box when he was completing a circuit.

Film. Louis Daguerre invented film when, having failed to produce an image on an iodized silver plate, he put the plate away in a cabinet filled with chemicals and the fumes from a spilled jar of mercury produced an image on the plate.

(Source: Mark A. Lemley, *The Atlantic* – June 15, 2012)

If you don't have a big enough goal, then certainly reviewing your mistakes is not going to be a favorite pastime.

Thomas Edison would never have invented a light bulb or Guglielmo Marconi the radio if they hadn't learned from their mistakes. And, since the only way to learn from a mistake is to make one, they eagerly made them. Why? Because the goal was so noble and big that they didn't let being wrong stop them.

Sara Blakely is the founder of Spanx and the youngest self-made female billionaire. She accredits her amazing success to her beloved father who followed a teaching of Wayne Dyer. When she was growing up her father would ask her each day: "So, what did you fail at today?" And as Sara mentions, "If there were no failures, Dad would be disappointed."

Why?

Because he knew, if there are no failures then she hadn't tried something outside her comfort zone.

The only person who can't learn is someone not willing to make mistakes.

Hillel used to say, "Someone who is afraid of being embarrassed cannot learn."
—Ethics of our fathers, 2:6

Learning from your mistakes doesn't have to involve publicizing them on Facebook. Keep a diary and ask a very simple question, "How could I have done today better?"

My teacher, Rabbi Weinberg Ztl, would ask himself this question every evening, "What could I have done to get more from today?" That simple question will have a huge impact on your life, as the 100,000 plus people who showed up for his funeral would surely attest.

It will also save you immense heartache, because you can be sure you will need that lesson in your future. And if you don't learn, you will certainly make the same mistake again.

This practice, when done regularly, is interestingly engaging. It's not the downer you might imagine. You can derive real energy and thrill from learning your own unique lessons from your own unique history.

If you lost $250,000 in the stock market, the personal pressure to deny and ignore is immense. And you will do exactly that if you don't want to be that rich. Whenever you encounter a person in denial, you are dealing with someone who doesn't have a big enough vision to get out of the way and learn.

Think of it this way: If you spent $250,000 on an exclusive business course, you would certainly do your best to apply those lessons.

Everything you can learn in life that's worth learning comes with a price tag; the lesson you learned from that stock market mistake was $250k. And it will feel totally worth it when, in the next investment round, you make $10m by applying the lesson. But you can only do that if you are willing to admit it, and learn from it.

Every mistake is your gold mine. Just dig.

Learn from the past—and if you do that, you really can change it!

I know, we have used a lot of ink explaining that the drive to change can be applied to the past or the present. In the present it is the recipe for winning, but in the past it is the recipe for disaster. It's what we call blame.

So allow me to explain.

It would be amazing to have a time machine. If it were possible, I too would go back and give myself this book just after I had learned to read! It would have saved me immense misery. But such devices only exist in movies.

However, this is what you can change about your past. If you truly learn from the past, then instead of the past being a regret, it will become a delight. And in that way you have transformed and changed the past—*because the lesson you learned will give you a tremendous advantage in the present.*

Let me explain this another way. How do you know you have learned from the past and not just glossed over and rationalized it?

If you love those mistakes!

This not as strange as you might imagine. Go meet an immigrant who is now a multi-billionaire and ask them the story of how they did it. They will tell you, with glee, all the people who ripped them off, the crazy ideas they tried that didn't work, and how those experiences taught them the ropes.

Read the biography of Warren Buffet, and try to calculate how successful he would be if he kept doing the same thing over and over again—without learning from his mistakes. Buffet, Washington, and Newton only became who they were because they were willing to admit and learn.

You can pretty much predict what you will become if you don't learn, but you can't if you do. It's beyond your imagination! The trajectory is enormous.

The world is waiting to see what your greatness and success will be like when you think like a winner.

CHAPTER 14
The Present: Fun

Mountains, buildings, and dirty socks tend to stay where you left them. But schedules, people, and the day do not.

As I wrote previously, a day is like the ocean; it's constantly in motion, and therefore it is never what you thought it would be. By the time you jot down your plans, the day is already different.

Adaption is the rule, and most people just don't get it. They don't stop grumbling and complaining. You hear them in the elevator in the morning, and they are there again on the train going home.

The weather wasn't what was forecast, lunch wasn't what they ordered, and the client didn't come through as they promised.

It's the classic battle of brain over emotions.

Our brains stay healthy through change and challenge. It's the curveball in any sport that makes it interesting. But emotions like consistency.

The trouble is that only the speed of light stays the same.

The present is always going to be different than what we planned, and there are only two attitudes anyone can have—excited or frustrated.

So, what's it gonna be?

Life doesn't let you know what is coming next. That's why there is news.

"Prediction is very hard, particularly when it's about the future."
—Yogi Berra

Human beings have no idea what is going to happen next, therefore being able to react meaningfully is the essence of youth and success. We all know people older than ourselves who get bent out of shape because the "All you can eat salad bar" is out of cucumbers. Or the grass wasn't cut like they wanted, or the latest gadget they ordered online is a day late.

If you want to stay young, then stay agile, not just in body, but in mind. Don't let your day be ruined by things that didn't go the way they should.

How do you do that?

As long as you don't get what you expect, then you will always be frustrated. Therefore, the only way to enjoy life is to get what you expect.

But what should you expect?

That today won't go the way you thought it would.

When you realize everything in life could just as easily go a completely different way, then you will never be disappointed.

"No battle plan ever survives contact with the enemy."
—Helmuth Karl Bernhard Graf von Moltke
Chief of Staff of the Prussian Army, 1800-1891

One of the saddest experiences I had when visiting Auschwitz was meeting a survivor. Understandably, and it's not appropriate to judge these heroes, he just couldn't deal with what had happened. He talked as though the war was still on.

Yet, I have met other survivors who had literally moved on. These people understand that life does not go the way you think it should, ever.

If you don't get that, then things far less than the Nazis invading Poland will ruin your day.

My teacher often told the story of the happy Dutch boy he met. The rabbi was an eager student of anyone who had something to teach, and he had to ask this young man, "Why are you so happy?"

The boy replied that he had been given the gift of happiness. He was riding his bicycle over a bridge in Holland, when a strong gust of wind blew him off. Right in front of a sand truck.

That truck severed his leg.

He described lying on the side of the road and seeing his leg some distance ahead.

He was obviously distressed, yet somehow he was able to say to himself, "This simply won't do."

He then described the scene in the hospital. His parents arrived and they were beside themselves, as we can well imagine.

Finally, he said to them, "Mom, Dad, you are going to have to get used to this."

To which they replied, "We have to get used to it?! No, you have to get used to it."

"No I don't," he answered, "I'm already used to it."

From then on he noticed with his friends that if things didn't go their way, they would get mad and upset. He, on the other hand, had learned he could get used to anything.

It's what he called "the gift of happiness."

Whether it's landing on Normandy Beach in 1944, or a day at Disneyland, it never goes according to plan. So you can spend a significant amount of time complaining, or you can try and figure how to respond like a winner—the latter is not only more effective, it's more fulfilling.

The Normandy Beach or severed leg examples might be extreme, but the principles are the same as in any business crisis or family predicament. What happens can't be planned for.

Stock brokerage firms make it very clear: Past experience is not an indicator of future performance. Which is a rather redundant statement, because other than concrete, nothing in life is predictable.

You can complain about it, and many do, but you can complain about the weather too. Neither makes a difference.

A complainer is no threat to a winner, because winners know that you can't complain and win too.

It's the reason you don't, or shouldn't, complain about anything on a job interview. Nothing speaks louder or more clearly that you are not winning material than a complaining attitude.

Life is unpredictable. The day you stop complaining about

life, is the day you increase your joy of life. This is the day you really start having fun. This is the day you start to win—at life.

CHAPTER 15
Summation

Synergy:
Everything You Need
to Know

Big Banks Know Their Past

To paraphrase George Santayana: "Those who don't learn from history don't have much to look forward to."

A neighbor borrows your lawn mower, then returns it broken and refuses to fix it.

Most annoying.

But where does that annoyance, which becomes an inner pain, go?

This is important, because there is only so much pain a person can absorb.

If you hold on to it, and that is how you deal with distressing interactions, then as your quota of pain gets filled, you will, by necessity, have to engage in greater avoidance.

Although this is quite understandable, and widely observable, it is nevertheless completely counterproductive.

As you collect more and more pain, your feelings of being abused will turn into equal proportions of cynicism. As the experience repeats itself, so the cynicism and distrust will mount.

If you continue to let these feelings build as you age, you will stop lending, and generally restrict yourself from all types of generosity and friendliness. It's why most people find their strongest friendships (and love) in their youth—it's when we are the least cynical.

But let's examine that whole scenario.

What was the reason for lending the lawn mower in the first place?

It feels good to be a good neighbor. A person might have had some hope their generosity would be reciprocated and noted, and would create some kind of warm neighborly experience.

But after the lawnmower is returned in seven different pieces, how does it feel now?

Animosity has replaced empathy.

But worse, every other neighbor will now be tainted with some kind of suspicion—even if it's just lightly. And that inkling of mistrust won't give anyone any warm feelings.

And this kind of reaction will intensify with every successive painful experience. A person becomes less and less excited about their future as it sinks in that humans are full of malice.

The pain caused by the bad neighbor has now spawned; it didn't go away just because it was ignored.

So what is the alternative?

Learn from how a bank makes loans.

Of course, we all think we have learned from the past. Ask any inmate of a maximum security prison and he will tell you he learned his lesson—even if that lesson was to have a faster getaway car.

So how do you know you have really learned, and not just become more cynical? After all, cynics think they have figured it out.

Simple.

When you are more excited about your future because of the lessons learned in your past.

Let me give an example.

On the morning of September 29, 1982, twelve-year-old Mary Kellerman died after taking potassium cyanide laced capsules from a bottle of Extra-Strength Tylenol. Eventually seven people in the Chicago region succumbed to the tampered product.

Before this, Tylenol had a 37 percent market share. Immediately after the cyanide poisonings, it was reduced to just 7 percent (Mitchell 1989).

Johnson & Johnson's reaction was unprecedented. They conducted an immediate product recall for the entire country, which amounted to about 31 million bottles and a loss of more than $100 million (Lazare, Chicago Sun-Times, 2002).

"Before 1982, nobody ever recalled anything," said Albert Tortorella, the public relations advisor for Johnson & Johnson (Source: *The New York Times*).

Considering the painkiller was Johnson & Johnson's best-selling product, this was a very bold move. And although Johnson & Johnson knew they were not responsible for the tampering, they nevertheless assumed responsibility for the public's safety.

By asking the question, "What do we learn from this?" they

caused the general public to feel more confident about Tylenol specifically, and Johnson & Johnson in general.

Disasters make the future brighter, if you are willing to learn the lesson. Johnson & Johnson didn't poison their own pills, and you didn't break your own lawnmower. Scale and size are not relevant. What is important is being able to keep doing what you want to do, whether that's curing headaches or making friends.

I don't wish to be Machiavellian here, but when done right disasters are opportunities to show off what you are truly made of.

We can well appreciate that many companies, in similar circumstances, would have gone on the attack and blamed the perpetrator (who was never found). After all, J&J did not do anything wrong and what was at stake was the bulk of their revenue and reputation. Similarly, you have every justification to get mad at the negligent neighbor who broke your mower.

We all find ourselves holding the bag to damage we didn't cause.

However, the consumer just wants the safest drug, and Johnson & Johnson had to demonstrate that they were looking out for their customers, not their own reputation. If that is your company credo, then a disaster will have the effect of making people feel more confident.

If anything, this is a reasonable indicator of success. One thousand dollars of Johnson & Johnson shares on September 28, 1982, just before the first Tylenol episode, would have been worth $22,062 in 2017, after four stock splits. (Source: *The New York Times*)

Yes, it's true, that looking out for the customer turns out to be best for the bottom line. But humans don't naturally react like that. Because the CEO is a real person too, and when it's your lawnmower that gets damaged, just like your pills, most of us react the same way—defensively.

But, if you really learn the lesson of Johnson & Johnson you will feel more confident about lending to your neighbor or selling a product like Tylenol.

However, cynicism is not how banks make money—they do their very best to figure out how to not make the same mistake again.

When a loan defaults, the bank doesn't say, "People are untrustworthy and we need to make it more difficult to borrow." Instead they try to discern the dynamics of what went wrong with the loan and apply it going forward.

The bank that can tease out the subtle differences between a good loan and a bad one is going to be very successful.

The road to your dream is paved with a multitude of mistakes. If you learn, then you will stop the calcium rich cynicism from lining the arteries of your heart.

The lender that can discern this critical lesson will not only continue to lend, but will actually feel even more confident about lending than they did the first time.

Motivation, fused with hard-earned lessons or wisdom, builds resolve.

If banks responded to lending the same way as our homeowner with the lawnmower, they would go out of business.

Instead each bad loan can be a lesson.

In the particular case of the lawnmower it might include some key questions, maybe even asking who will be responsible if it breaks. The specifics here may not apply to you. We've all been burned trusting the wrong person in a variety of situations. However, the general rule does apply: Don't let bad experiences taint your good intentions.

"Above all else, guard your heart, for life comes from it." —King Solomon, Proverbs 4:23

NASA Knows the Present

Why does peace of mind seem so elusive?

Because peace of mind comes from enjoying your challenges—as they are happening.

That probably sounds somewhat counter intuitive. That's because our picture of peace of mind includes a hammock and a beer, and it wouldn't hurt to have a spectacular Caribbean beach either.

How can you have peace of mind and be engaged in a challenge?

Let's examine this dynamic.

On January 27, 1967, three astronauts tragically died in their Apollo 1 vehicle while still on the launchpad. In the aftermath NASA did a lot of soul searching and self-examination.

But what is most relevant is that they eagerly welcomed criticism.

Why?

Because they loved what they were doing.

Do you have that attitude with your life? Do you welcome criticism?

If the answer is no, it's probably because you aren't really that excited about being successful. If you were, you would want to know how you can improve.

If the goal is important to you, then you will love the process, warts and all.

But if the goal is not important, then all you will love is being free of it, and any problem or delay that comes along will just add to the frustration.

It's easy to tell what parts of a person's life they love and what parts they barely tolerate. Give them advice or criticism and you will see. If they write it down, that's a great indicator of enthusiasm. If they get defensive, or just show polite interest, it generally means you've touched on one of their "necessary evils."

When you are doing what you love, you love the challenge. That's peace of mind.

I spend a lot of time on long train rides traveling to speaking engagements. I meet some very interesting people. The other day I was sitting opposite a guy who works for Amtrak. He's one of the people with a hard hat who fixes the lines. It's tough and challenging work.

I asked him what he did and we had a great time talking about the ins and outs and dangers of working the line. I honestly have virtually no interest in how trains work. I know some people love it, but it's not my cup of tea. Even with that, this guy kept my interest the entire time talking about trains—because his love of what he does was infectious. He saw every day as one filled with opportunity. He was engaged.

And he had peace of mind.

When you love what you do, peace of mind is what you have.

The Dentist Knows the Future

Imagine for a moment being in the dentist chair awaiting a long and almost certainly painful procedure, despite what the dentist has told you.

Add to that picture a great tomorrow. You're getting married, maybe taking your company public, your first child is due, or you are off to your dream vacation. In this kind of situation the dentist visit becomes much more tolerable—maybe even mildly amusing.

Why is this?

Because whatever is going on in your present, no matter how distasteful, will become much more acceptable if you can picture yourself in a great future.

And the opposite is also true.

A bland or even dire future will make even the smallest irritants unbearable. In this scenario, any slight deviation from a perfect day can easily send you into a tailspin of negativity.

I have a friend who told me this story. One of his high school teachers was an officer on a ship in Pearl Harbor on that fateful day in 1941 when Japan launched a surprise attack on the U.S. naval base. His boat was hit and he found himself in the ocean.

His only choice was to swim to shore. Unfortunately, it was a long swim, and he soon found himself exhausted. Eventually he couldn't go on, and so he closed his eyes and went down. Much to his surprise, however, after a few inches down he touched the ocean floor. He realized he must be close to shore, even though he couldn't see it. So he pushed himself up and managed to make it home safely.

This is the question.

Why did he give up in the first place? He clearly had enough energy to make it. He really was not completely out of steam. The answer is because he could not see his future.

Once he realized how close he was, then he found the energy to keep on going.

The times when things come together for that moment where life just works and the world is set aright are exceedingly rare. Most of the time we have to tolerate varying degrees of annoyance. Nothing as bad as being in the middle of the ocean during a battle; at least I hope not. It's all much more banal than that—too hot, too cold, the news is bad, the Internet too slow, the boss chewed you out for no reason, and your back is hurting.

If you let it get to you, then it's easy to slip into a crazy world of constant victimhood. And many people engage in varying degrees of that malady.

However, no matter what you are going through, when you imagine a bright future, then your pain will dissipate.

This is an absolute: Anyone who lets the annoyances of life get to them, no matter how dramatic those annoyances are, has no vision of tomorrow—at least not a good one.

There is always something going wrong, and sometimes it's more than one thing. But the best medicine is a great tomorrow.

The closer your picture of the future is to perfect, one so bright you can barely wait, then the more the present will live up to its name.

Part 4
CHAPTER 16
Bad Attitude

A dvice comes in four basic categories.

The first three are easy to understand: Good advice, bad advice, and advice that's a complete waste of time.

Let me give some examples of waste of time advice.

Doubtless you have been a recipient (or maybe even a perpetrator) of one of these little gems.

"Drive safely."

Regardless of an abundance of contrary evidence, most teenagers think they are safe drivers. Therefore, it is an act of pure fantasy to expect the words, "Drive safely" to rest on any part of your child's cerebral cortex.

"Drink responsibly."

Really? Isn't that a bit of an oxymoron?

"Think outside the box."

Really? Like people want to be closed-minded? I have had the dubious pleasure of meeting more than my fair share of chronically closed-minded people, none of whom imagined that was their affliction.

But my favorite piece of waste of time advice is "Have a nice day."

"Well, thank you so much, I was just about to saw half my foot off with a rusty chainsaw, but thanks to you, I've changed my mind."

The reason we like these little gems of futility is because we have to balance these two absolutes of life:

We like giving advice.

We hate offending people.

For example, your co-worker has an oral hygiene deficiency. So by telling them they need to brush their teeth more frequently, or just frequently, you are also pointing out their breath stinks. And you don't necessarily want to go there.

And because this scenario engages the two absolutes of life, most people just hold their nose and don't say anything.

And then there is the fourth type of advice: The painfully necessary.

In this category almost nothing is more offensive, and ubiquitously necessary, than "improve your attitude."

It's rare to find someone who couldn't benefit from an uptick in this department. At the same time, most people are blithely unaware of how dour their attitude really is.

This state of affairs can be compared to a popular apocryphal story of the man who wanted to learn archery. After much research he located the world's greatest archer, who offered him the choice of two courses. One would cost a small fortune and would take three years to complete. The other was only $25 and could be finished in approximately thirty minutes.

After contemplating these two choices, our man decides on

the thirty-minute course. Archery wasn't as important to him as he first imagined.

The master archer is clearly insulted by the poor choice of his new apprentice, but nevertheless he beckons him to a nearby field for the first, and only, lesson.

In the field stood a large barn. Pointing to its massive doors, and handing the student a bow and arrow, he asked: "Do you think you can hit the door?"

"Yes," the student replied confidently, thinking to himself, "I can show him I am not a complete incompetent." He aimed his weapon, pulled back on the string and then released. Swish and then thud as the arrow flew perfectly toward the barn and made its target.

The student stood back proudly. But the master simply walked over to the barn and grabbed a can of paint from inside. Taking a brush, he painted a bright red circle around the arrow.

Turning to the student he proclaimed, "Completed." And walked away, leaving the puzzled student to just stare at the arrow in the bullseye and take in the deeper lesson just imparted.

There are two ways to get a bullseye. One is to practice and perfect, work and toil.

The other is to simply draw a circle around wherever you are.

Having a great attitude is a great way to live. But unless you fit into the category of the very few people who don't need improvement, then you, my dear reader, need an adjustment.

The problem is, how do you do it?

Most people have no idea how to make such a change.

And although there are truisms galore—"Life is good"; "Always look on the bright side of life"; or "It could always get worse"—such sayings just don't seem to make any impact.

Therefore, rather than be frustrated, it's easier to just paint a circle around the spot where you are standing and declare "Completed!" This will explain why many, if not most people believe they have a great attitude—even if they clearly don't.

The truth is, a great attitude is the most important factor for achieving success. You can pretend all you want, but without actually having one you are not going anywhere. At least nowhere you really want to go. It's like having pretend money—great until you actually want to buy something. You can pretend you are a master archer, but without training you'll never hit a bullseye.

A great attitude will enable you to overcome any obstacle and achieve any goal. A pretend one only works until you finally get up in the morning. From that point on you are sunk.

It is not just coincidence that "attitude" and "altitude" are only one letter apart. You can't shoot further or dream higher than your attitude.

Attitude is rocket fuel. What is in the tank will determine the altitude of the spaceship. Similarly, we can't achieve goals higher than our attitude.

The reason people fall short is they don't have the attitude that will allow them to reach the goals they really want. And simply chanting "I believe in me" just doesn't cut it.

Whatever your attitude level, your goals won't exceed that limit. Thus, you need to raise your attitude to attain the life you really want.

That's how to live life.

That's living real.

That's winning.

And that's what this last part of the book is going to give you.

CHAPTER 17
Back to the Future

Let's go back to that best day of your life that we talked about previously. For the sake of simplicity, we are going to give that day a value of 10. And thus 1 is the value of a really, really bad day.

Now, using the best day as your base line, I want you to give a number for yesterday. Think about it and don't read on without writing it in the box on the next page.

Then, give a number for today. Again, think about it and write it down.

Now consider this, realistically, what number do you feel tomorrow is going to be?

Take a few minutes to think and then write the number in. Obviously you don't know what it's really going to be like, but what is your feeling? What does your gut tell you. Is it going to be a 10, or a 1, or something in-between?

Don't read on until you have completed this task.

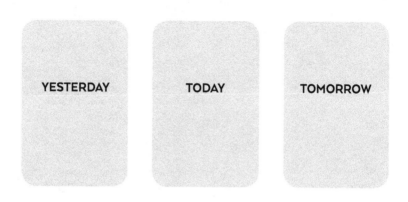

This is what it all means:

If the number for tomorrow is less than 10, then you are in need of a serious attitude adjustment.

As we demonstrated before, how you think about tomorrow is what makes today what it is. The number you have for tomorrow is a very accurate description of what kind of day you are having right now.

If you think tomorrow is going to be a 10, or maybe even some number off the scale, like a 15 or 20, you will be so excited you won't be able to sleep tonight. Alternatively, if tomorrow is a 3, then almost certainly you'll need some help getting up in the morning.

That number represents your attitude. Therefore, raising that number is the priority of your life because nothing else is going to make the difference you want in your life.

Attitude is the most important part of your psyche. Your ability to function all comes down to your attitude. When it dips too low it's hard to even make a cup of coffee; and when it's really high, you don't need one.

Nothing is more magnetic than a phenomenal attitude.

And even though you might think your number only exists in your mind, it really doesn't. It is plastered all over your face and engraved between your eyes. Everyone can read your number as clearly as the price of a gallon in front of a gas station, because the difference between a 3 and a 10 is not only dramatic, it's obvious.

The only reason (more) people are not telling you what your number is, is the same reason you aren't telling your co-worker to brush his teeth.

But the truth is this: Their lack of telling is actually telling.

You have certainly had times in your life when things went really well and your attitude was sky high. And you probably noticed how many people commented on it.

Well, from that you can infer that if people are not commenting on your attitude now, then it's because it is less than stellar.

I am sure you have been in the office when someone walked in with an incredibly great attitude because something has them all fired up with positive energy. Perhaps they just got a promotion and are dying to tell everyone, maybe they won the lottery or just got engaged; whatever the reason, their number is obvious. When someone is a 10 it's as plain as day, and the only thing you don't know about them is why.

It's also obvious in the other extreme too, meaning if their number dips below 5, everyone can see it on their face. The difference is you have to be pretty bold to ask why this time.

So whether people are formally pointing it out to you or not, either way, you need to push that number up because it reflects your attitude, motivation, and ultimately, success—because goals cannot exceed attitude.

It's important to emphasize that there is no such thing as faking it. You might be able to fake an expensive handbag or a Swiss watch, but you can't fake attitude—if it isn't real it isn't there.

Especially with people who know you best.

There is a real palpable difference between a genuinely great attitude and everything else. And everyone knows it.

The bottom line is this, only a truly great attitude can create sustained motivational living. And only such an attitude can get you to have the life you really want.

To summarize: Raising that number is the most important job of your life.

Two more points on attitude:

Your number is never static. Just because yesterday was a 10 has very little to do with today. Each day is independent.

I am sure you have experienced many great days followed by disasters. You can't rely on yesterday to make today great—you can only use tomorrow to improve today.

The second point is there is an inverse relationship between your age and the number you have for tomorrow, meaning the younger you are the higher tomorrow is going to be.

The opposite is also true!

I am sorry to tell you this, but it's a downward slope toward zero. Your number for tomorrow is inevitably only going down from what it was a year or a decade ago—unless you work on it.

It's why we like spending time with children, their tomorrow number is usually very high and therefore they have a phenomenal attitude.

Age really takes a toll because the older we get, the more we think the future will be dark. And the more negative we are about the future, the lower our attitude becomes.

As such, the younger a person, the brighter the future. You might dismiss this as youthful naiveté, and you might be right, but that naiveté has a tremendous health benefit. We feel, and usually are, in better shape when we have a great attitude. It's also, as I have been explaining, the key to success. It simply cannot be underestimated.

Thus I have to mention one of those painfully important pieces of advice: Unless you work on improving your attitude today, you aren't going to like your attitude tomorrow.

When we were seven years old we thought we were always going to be super positive, forever. We didn't understand why people much older than us just didn't get how fun life is. But then we become those older people, and what do we do? We look at people even older than us with a disdain that's similar to when we were seven.

We don't seem to get it that those older people with the awful attitude are our time machine—we are looking at ourselves in the future.

We tend to think we can maintain our attitude level whether we are seven, seventeen, or seventy. It never quite dawns on us that there is a trend here, and it's not moving in the direction we want.

We live in the most technological era ever. So many aspects of our lives defy the norms of our ancestors: Light in the evening, heat in the winter, flying through the sky, instant sharing. Surely we can reverse the attitude trend too?

For sure we can!

CHAPTER 18

The Good Old Days

L et me take you back to my high school, an all-boys private school in London.

In those days, the headmaster would walk the halls, cane in hand, in eager anticipation of a boy in need. Our English teacher was an Oxford-trained mastermind, mild in disposition and well versed in the ways of school boys.

His generation saw the First World War and reveled in the glow, albeit dimming, of the British Empire. It was common for people his age to extoll their childhood as "the good old days." It was the ultimate one-upmanship, something at which the British work very hard.

And yet, relative to the life my teacher had growing up, it was we, the new generation, that were really living the dream life. The quality of life was unmatched in the history of humanity. Technology, health, and wealth were so much greater than anything previous. And so it annoyed me to no end when people of that generation would tell us that it was they who really had it good.

Why did it irk me so?

Because there was nothing that I could find in that history to justify such fond reminisces.

You are probably going to think this odd, but I concluded: My English teacher must be right.

Why?

Because no matter who I asked, whatever their age, their pasts were always "the good old days."

This led me to the most paradoxical conclusion that one day in my future I, too, will look back at this present as the "good old days."

But this was also frustrating. There was nothing in my present that made me feel wondrous in the way my elders described their youth.

What's more, the time that many of them were referring to as their good old days was The Blitz of London! Which, by all accounts, were some of the darkest days of Europe. In pure quality of life, their latter days were much better than their former.

So how could their past be the good old days, and not their present?

It took me four decades to figure it out, but this will explain it: Youth places a high value on the future, which, as we have explained, makes that time in the present, great.

That mechanism can make any time great, no matter how bad it really is. It's like the day your parents announce you're going to Disneyland. It's the day you get engaged, the day you win the lottery. That day becomes phenomenal, because it's packed with the expectation of a great future. No matter what kind of day it really was.

Sometimes it's even better than the actual future you are

expecting.

That teacher had fond memories of his youth because at that time he looked forward to his future.

And even though those earlier days were really terrible, and his latter days great, it makes no difference—it's his youth that he misses.

When he finally got to that anticipated future, there was now little to look forward to.

Thus, by default, the older people get, the less they enjoy their present. Even though this, the present, is the tomorrow they were always looking forward to!

I know this is complicated, but it really is key to your success, so please excuse me as I try to restate it another way so that it will be clearer.

Let's say you just got off a plane with your wife and two year old child. The county you are coming from is Russia, Haiti, Sudan, Ethiopia (you name it), you literally don't have a penny and even though you were a doctor in your home country, you have to make a living cutting grass. Your wife (who was a teacher back home) cleans bathrooms so your daughter can have books for school.

No matter what the weather, you could be hungry and freezing cold, but as far as you are concerned, the day you touched down at JFK airport will be remembered as the best day of your life.

Not the day you get your first job, not the day you make your first million dollars! Not even the day you buy a yacht. These events pale compared to that day you arrived in the U.S. For this simple reason—on that day the future was glowing, blazing bright.

No matter how good, or how bad your day is, it's the future that makes your day

What does all this mean, practically?

In ten years from now, your number for tomorrow is going to be less than your current number for tomorrow. This will have the effect that when you look back you will realize how happy you are now.

Even though you don't perceive yourself as so happy.

Those who were children in London during World War II worked very hard at making their future lives better, and by all accounts they succeeded gloriously. We live in the world that they created, and it's far better than the world they were born into. Yet, it's their youth that they miss.

Do you realize what happened here? They didn't end up enjoying life more, even though their lives were better.

You too, are not going to enjoy the world you are desperately trying to create, as much as the life you have now.

This is the mistake that people make in what is commonly called a mid-life crisis.

A mid-life crisis is the moment a person realizes that all their efforts at reversing this downhill trend have been for naught.

This is the incredible paradox of life: The more miserable our lives are, the more we have to look forward to. The more we have to look forward to, then the greater our attitude and motivation.

But paradoxically, the better our lives become, then the opposite happens—we have less to look forward to, which adversely impacts our motivation and attitude.

This is the new immigrant experience: When they step into

their new country, their worldly possessions may add up to nothing more than a small suitcase, but it's not what's in their suitcase that counts. It's what's in their hearts. Their future is very bright.

Eventually, when they reach the pinnacle of success and sit down with their grandchildren to tell them how tough it was when they came to this country, they will do so with a sparkle in their eye as they recall those glorious times with fond nostalgia.

"Ah, those were the good old days!" they will tell their youthful descendants. And their grandchildren will wonder, just like I did, what is grandpa talking about?

In the building where I teach, the cleaning crew sometimes brings their kids with them to help. Those kids have a brighter attitude than most kids. The mistake is thinking that if they had an easier life, and didn't have to clean buildings too, they would achieve so much more! But, if anything, by making their lives easier they'd likely achieve less.

I am all for alleviating people's suffering, and am in no way advocating that we should actively keep people in poverty. In fact, it's a duty on us all to lighten everyone's load in whatever way we can. But hope in the future is one of the most powerful forces to alleviate any hardship.

In all likelihood, if you own this book then you are living the good life. If you earn more than approximately $33,000 annual income you are in the top one percent of the richest people on this planet (source: www.globalrichlist.com). You can't get much better than that. And if you make over $70,000 you are in the top 0.1 percent.

I have nothing against improving people's living conditions. It's a lovely thing to enjoy life, but increasing the quality of your life does not necessarily equate to an equal amount of enthusiasm for that life. If anything, and much to many people's chagrin, it's an inverse relationship.

As I wrote above, the new immigrant has an incredible day on the day he arrives, simply because he foresees a great future. But as he inches closer toward that future, he proportionately loses his excitement.

People engage in the most futile attempts at avoiding this rule.

Denial can keep you going for a long time, and substance abuse can stretch it out a little longer, but eventually everyone over the age of approximately thirty-five will have to face, in some form of awareness or another, that they enjoyed life a lot more when they were kids.

Don't mistake my words, few of us want to go back to living as we did, and even if we could, that is not the solution. Even my English teacher, and for sure the immigrant, will agree to that.

It's not the things that we had then that we miss, it's the things we foresaw and expected to have that gave us our excitement. This is what we are missing now.

Trading your mini-van for a red Ferrari is not going to have any greater impact on your life than when you got your mini-van in the first place. It's not a change in your outer world that is in need, but the inner one.

How, you ask?

Dabo Swinney is currently the head coach of a top college football team. The *Washington Post* called him, "One of the game's most talented and magnetic young coaches."

Swinney explains how he transformed his team, when they "changed from the inside, it blossomed on the outside. You can't ever do it the other way. . . . Until you get the inside of you right, your outer is never going to be right." (Source: *The Bleacher Report* and thanks to Rabbi Yaakov Singer)

Think back to when you were six years old, the idea that tomorrow you were going to Disneyland gave tomorrow an incalculably high number. At whatever age you are now, going to Disneyland is no longer going to have that same impact.

Why?

Because you've been to Disneyland, and the real thing is rarely as exciting as the fantasy.

As a student told me when he got his first Porsche: "Owning one is nice, but the anticipation was better."

You just can't replay that movie again and enjoy it the same way.

Once you've tasted it and realized it isn't that great, then you cannot recreate that anticipation. And it's the anticipation that gives life its excitement and thrill.

Simply put, there is nothing you can do today to make today great. To make today great you need a phenomenal tomorrow.

And that is what you miss about your youth, a fantastic over-the-top incredible future.

I often speak around the country, and whenever possible I like to take one of my children. It's great bonding time. My daughter recently told me that when she was much younger she was so excited to go on one of those trips that she couldn't sleep the night before.

But when I recently asked her if she wants to come along

now, she had to decline. It isn't that she didn't want to go, she did. But she didn't want to go enough to rearrange her life. Don't worry, I get it, it's not about me. She is older. She needs bigger things to keep her up at night. She has a great life— she's happy and really enjoys her job—and I am sure, as you are reading this, you probably have a great life too. But there is nothing like having something in your life that is so exciting you can hardly sleep at night in anticipation.

The whole point here is to maintain the good in your life you have attained so far, and notch it up a few numbers. Don't chase experiences that can't improve your life. Don't give up everything good in your life for a fantasy. And certainly seek advice from the most thoughtful people you can find.

Don't ruin the good you already have. But let's get that "going to Disneyland" anticipation back.

We used to know how to do that—let's do it again!

CHAPTER 19

The Disappointment Trap

I love my wife.

I love my house. And oh, I also love my new slippers.

Does that mean the way I feel about my wife is the same as my slippers?

Absolutely not.

When it comes to emotions, the English language is extremely vague and wooly.

Colors, measurements, and objects are precise, but the world of feelings is like living in a world reduced to primary colors. Love, hate, happy, angry, and sad are about all we have to describe a multitude of feelings.

We can sum up our financial day with a very exact number and then relay it on a chart relative to other days and other people. When we want to describe our financial state we can use a range of terms—liquid or hard assets, plus a vast array of financial instruments. But try telling anyone how your day is going and it's usually reduced to terms like "good" or "bad."

This obviously leads to an immense amount of inaccuracy

in both diagnosis and treatment. Even though we use the term unhappy to describe every displeasure, there is a great difference between real unhappiness and disappointment. And the inaccuracy is dangerous.

Invariably when people use the word unhappy, what they really mean is disappointed.

Contrary to the common perception, unhappiness doesn't make you quit your marriage, or even your job, or do any other significant act that would upend the status quo.

Despite what you might hear in the media, unhappiness is quite tolerable—it's disappointment that is debilitating.

Let me explain.

If your displeasure with life reaches the point where you are willing to significantly impact and risk everything you have, then you are not acting out of unhappiness, it's really disappointment that is forcing your hand.

Why?

Most people have jobs that don't make them happy. What I mean is, given the choice most people would rather not work. But if they have to work, then they find their particular job perfectly tolerable.

Let me demonstrate.

If you inherited $300 million dollars, then how long would it take you to quit your job? People who are happy with what they are doing generally don't stop doing it.

For example, if you inherited millions of dollars would you stop playing golf or eating steaks?

Why not?

Because you like those things—they make you happy. If work made us happy, then you would find a significant number of people doing it for free, and I've yet to meet anyone doing that!

What is really going on here?

As I have been trying to explain, we can tolerate unhappiness, and often do. A person who feels an urge to quit is not doing so because they are unhappy, it's because they are disappointed. They might call it unhappy, but that's because English is very inaccurate.

Here is the insight: Human beings are made in such a way that we can tolerate unhappiness.

That's why many of us can spend a majority of our day doing all kinds of mind-numbing activities in the pursuit of a goal. Human beings don't need constant immediate pleasure. It's great if it happens, we just don't need it to survive.

It's like going on vacation. You can spend a lot of boring and unpleasant time getting to the dream spot. And even though the process of getting there is uncomfortable, it's completely acceptable, because, as we have been pointing out, human beings are built in such a way that we can ignore the negative in the pursuit of a worthy goal.

We can, and often do, tolerate being unhappy.

Unhappiness is very bearable.

In fact, unhappiness is so tolerable that most people don't realize they are even in a state of unhappiness. In fact, they think this is the way it is supposed to be.

Most people don't love their job, they don't love their car, don't love their home, don't love their weight, they don't love a multitude of aspects of their existence. Given the choice they would all opt for something else.

But these are not the things people are complaining about.

What people complain about are not the things that make them unhappy. Rather, it's the things that give them disappointment that are the cause to complain.

It's like the person who buys a Rolls Royce and finds out the ashtrays don't open properly. After spending over a month on the phone with customer support, they finally ask him "Do you smoke?"

"No," he replies. "But this car cost me half a million dollars and I expect the ashtrays to work!"

Obviously he isn't unhappy because the ashtrays don't work—he doesn't even need them.

Rather, he's disappointed.

It's disappointment (and not unhappiness), that will make him waste his time on something that makes no difference in his life.

Alternatively, you save up enough money to buy your first car. As such you are thrilled that for $350 the windows go up and down.

The Ross Dress for Less clothing chain uses this concept as its business strategy. As anyone who has shopped there can testify, the racks of clothes in their stores are very poorly organized. This is not a mistake. They specifically want it that way so the customer feels excited about uncovering a real find.

In other words, they know you are walking into the store expecting to be disappointed, and they use that so you will become pleasantly surprised.

Ross has successfully built the upending of disappointment into the shopping experience. The same "bargain" if displayed prominently would not feel as great as when the customer "accidentally" finds it hidden in the mess.

Among cell phone users the group with the highest satisfaction rates are the customers that buy pre-paid phones, even though these phones tend to have the least features.

The reason is that cell phone companies have painted themselves into a corner. They have promised a phone experience they can't deliver, so just about everyone is disappointed. The only people who are not disappointed are the pre-paid customers because their experience is actually more than they expected.

But consider this, anyone with a smart phone today is holding more computer power in their hand than the entire Allied Forces of World War II. You can't be unhappy with that.

And you aren't—you are disappointed. You thought you were getting something even better.

Let us say you have dreamt of visiting Paris since you were a small child. Finally, after many years, you have the opportunity to take your dream vacation. Your itinerary is planned to the minute. It includes dining at the best restaurants, visiting historic sites, and of course a few days at the Louvre.

Unfortunately, the plane is packed solid, the air conditioning isn't working properly, and the entertainment system crashes. The food is cold and stale, and the attendants are rude. This is unhappiness.

But you can tolerate this.

However, five minutes after you check in, your hotel experiences a major flood and every guest is relocated to a sub-standard hovel, where you get food poisoning at the first meal. Then riots break out in the streets, and all the public attractions are closed because a state of emergency is declared.

You will never forget that vacation.

And even though you will probably keep flying, there is a good likelihood that you'll never visit Paris again.

Disappointment is so debilitating we will do just about anything to avoid it, including lowering our expectations.

This is what I call "The Disappointment Trap."

Thinking you can lower your expectations to avoid disappointment and enjoy life more is the path to oblivion.

Take a look at this diagram:

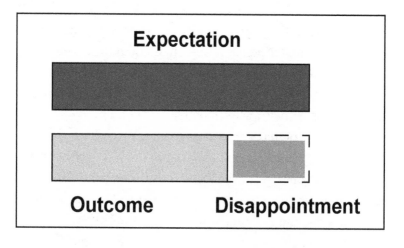

The seemingly simple way to resolve this issue is to lower expectations to match the outcome. The problem is, this diagram is an absolute. Meaning, if expectations are 100, then outcome will be 80, and disappointment will be 20.

But, if expectations are 80, the outcome does not stay the same; it drops too. Yes, disappointment is also less—but it's still there.

On top of that, outcome doesn't drop by the same percentage as your lowered expectations—it's actually greater. Meaning if you lower expectations to 80, then outcome is not 64; it could be as low as 50. Or worse.

Why? Because when you lower your expectations, you lower your effort too, which is a key factor in output.

What is imosst mportant to realize is this: You can't improve your life through lowering your expectations.

Life never exceeds expectations.

Life, and for sure winning, is all about having the right expectations. And they have to be high to create motivation.

Expectations are uplifting. If you expect tomorrow to be a 10 you are going to have a great day today. How could it be otherwise? You have a great tomorrow to look forward to.

Expectations are all about being so excited about the future you willingly increase your efforts. It's a belief that your future is real and phenomenal.

Therefore, expectations need to be understood to avoid the disappointment trap.

For example, you just don't show up on the first day of work and become the CEO, even though that's how it goes in the movies.

You don't just say "I do" and live happily ever after, even though that's how it goes in the movies. You don't show up at the gym and come out looking like Dwayne Johnson or Sylvester Stallone, even though that's how it goes in the movies.

As ridiculous as these expectations are, you only know they are absurd because you probably learned the hard way. And that hard way usually results in the lowering of expectations.

What we should do, however, when our expectations are not met, is to re-evaluate those expectations—not lower them.

That is the mistake of the disappointment trap. And it's tragic.

The disappointment trap happens when you think life will

be better with lower expectations. So you lower your expectations thinking you can avoid disappointment.

Rule of Life #1: Disappointment cannot be avoided.

Rule of Life #2: Having low expectations is even worse than disappointment.

Your life was exciting when you had a great expectation. You are not going to recreate that life with anything but an expectation of equal magnitude.

People lower their expectations because they don't realize this simple fact: You can't have a great life without great expectations.

Yes, disappointment is a downer. But avoiding disappointment by lowering your expectations won't give you the phenomenal life you had when your expectations were great. When you decide on a goal based on the need to avoid disappointment, your anticipation for tomorrow will only trend lower.

Let me show you what low expectations look like: *Take a visit to your local nursing home. You will find just about everyone walking around with low expectations, including the staff.*

It's so infectious you simply can't stay there too long. You can feel the disease of low expectations trying to invade your mind.

This is one of the primary reasons we feel uncomfortable in places like that. We can sense the low expectations creeping into our psyche.

It's expectations that define who we are and how we operate. We become very different people depending on how low or high our expectations are.

Have you ever attended a high school reunion only to be shocked at meeting an old friend twenty years later whose life has been sucked out of them because they kept lowering their expectations at each disappointment?

We start out life very, very excited. Anticipation is high and our goals are Moon Shot material. Eventually and inevitably, disappointment hits and we enter phase two of our lives.

Up until then we didn't need to consider our goals—we were guided and coached by parents who ensured our success. We were usually picked for a team, and were placed in the appropriate class to match our skills so our grades were never that bad. And, if anything didn't turn out right, someone was there to show us how to fix it.

But when we went out on our own and our parents were no longer there to guide and protect us, disappointment hit— and it hit hard. Nothing prepared us for this.

Naturally, we don't want to experience that again, so we make the mistake of lowering our goals. This is the disappointment trap.

With this, the excitement dissipates immediately because our goal has fundamentally changed: It now includes avoiding disappointment, which is far from inspiring.

If yesterday your goal was to fly the Atlantic, and today it's to avoid being disappointed, then you are going to find it hard to get up tomorrow!

What's more, whatever you do, disappointment keeps happening. You simply cannot eliminate it from life, despite all your best efforts to the contrary.

When you realize your first job is not a piece of cake, or you discover marriage is not a Disney movie, or that the gym is more painful than you thought, staying just as excited and motivated is only going to happen if you know what to do with the disappointment.

Understanding disappointment so it doesn't impact your emotional equilibrium is the key. It is going to be a most valuable gem in your arsenal of wisdom.

The people who can do this have an emotional shield that protects them as they steam through their careers. They never lower their goals because they never need to.

It's like being a tank in battle, regular bullets just bounce off and the tank keeps on going.

This is not about being callous or cruel. As we will come to see, it's really extremely sensitive. But it is key to winning, because your motivation is shielded. Disappointment just doesn't get through.

This is grit!

"If you're going through hell, keep going."
—Winston Churchill

CHAPTER 20
Inevitable Disappointment

Animals do a very limited number of things. But they do them incredibly well.

And they do them over and over again.

And that's it.

Giraffes aren't trying to swing from trees because they saw the monkeys do it. And monkeys aren't trying to chase zebra's because they saw the lions do it. And lions aren't trying to fly because they saw the eagles do it.

Animals know what they are, what they can do, and they practice it all to perfection.

Human beings don't.

We are not (naturally) very good at anything. Sorry! And the bare trifle of things we are negligibly proficient at is often abandoned to try new things.

There is one exception.

The one thing that humans do exclusively well, and animals don't even come close to is this:

We dream.

We dream big.

We plan great futures.

Whether it's Thomas Jefferson in 1776 or Harry Truman after World War II, Mahatma Gandhi during the British rule or Nelson Mandela in South Africa, these men, and multitudes like them, pictured a better tomorrow.

There is one big problem with dreaming big however.

Disappointment.

Big disappointment.

Disappointment, I am sorry to tell you, not only stings—it's absolutely inevitable.

Why?

Because you just can't dream and then the next day live happily ever after.

You can't dream and get it right.

Ever!

NASA has more PhDs per computer terminal than any other enterprise in the world, and they still get it wrong. The reality never fits the dream the first time around.

Disappointment is therefore incredibly ubiquitous. No one escapes it.

It's also absolutely necessary.

Why?

Because disappointment is the cost of entry to winning.

It's not only winners that dream big. Everyone dreams big.

It's how they handle disappointment that separates the winners and everyone else.

It's not the dream that separates the winners, it's what happens when the inevitable failure happens and the resulting disappointment sets in.

When it doesn't work out, the winner figures out why, and tries again. Everyone else finds a lower goal.

"You just can't beat the person who never gives up."
—Babe Ruth

Disappointment separates the winners from the rest of humanity. Winners are willing to be disappointed, and everyone else isn't.

What does everyone else do instead?

They choose safe goals that are way beneath their potential. This is the disappointment trap we mentioned earlier.

When people say you need realistic goals, what they really mean is that you need to lower your goals. Because (they believe) if you lower your expectations you will avoid disappointment.

This is a colossal mistake.

A human being has an incredible ability to project a world that not only does not exist, but most importantly it also does not logically connect with any reality past or present. This is the definition of a dream.

Dreams, by definition, are never realistic.

As such, no computer could imagine or plot where your inspiration and imagination might take you. Even a consultant is of no help because they are working out of a playbook that contains only what has already happened.

Henry Ford famously said, "If I asked my customers what they want, they would ask for a faster horse."

Can you imagine what a consultant would advise Steve

Jobs while he was creating his first computer in his garage? We are all grateful Jobs could not afford such a luxury.

I am in no way advocating recklessness. But when failure inevitably hits, what we need to do is not lower our expectations, but understand how to manage the disappointment.

This is what winners do!

In the history of the world, no one has ever achieved anything of any significance on the first try. Furthermore, a bare modicum of research will reveal that if any achiever of high success had used their failures to lower their ambition, such failures would have reduced their goals in life to nothing more than opening their eyes in the morning.

"It takes 20 years to make an overnight success."
—Eddie Cantor
A superstar of early 20th Century radio, stage, and film.

Why is this so important?

Because life never exceeds expectations.

There is no fun or excitement in a goal that is realistic.

If you are not willing to be disappointed, you will never be thrilled with life.

"Success consists of going from failure to failure without loss of enthusiasm."
—Winston Churchill

CHAPTER 21
The Fountain of Youth

"Never allow the fear of striking out keep you from playing the game."
—Babe Ruth

Show me a team that isn't disappointed in losing, and I will show you a team that will never win.

Babe Ruth knew he wasn't going to hit every ball out of the ballpark. But he sure didn't play that way.

No one becomes a winner by expecting to lose.

Think of your life like a batter at the plate waiting to be pitched the perfect ball. That ball could be a great business deal, job offer, date, friendship, new customer … anything.

The problem is, you don't know which ball it will be.

This is what Babe Ruth and every other winner understands. No one knows.

One in twenty balls has the potential for being the big hit you've been waiting for, but you will never find that one by waiting for it to be obvious. You have to have patience and deal with the disappointment later.

Similarly, one in twenty business deals has the potential for being the big deal, but you will never find it unless you examine each and every one. That doesn't mean invest in each one blindly. It means investigate each one like this could be the biggie.

The stories are rife with those who bought Berkshire Hathaway in the early days, or Apple when Jobs was young, the same for INTEL and Amazon. But the stories less told are of those people who turned Buffet down and who thought Jeff Bezos was crazy.

I heard of an investor who rejected Facebook, another who thought Velcro was a bad idea, and another who sold his Apple stock way too early.

It's hard to pick a winner, but it's harder still if your investment strategy is to avoid disappointment.

The future belongs to those who believe in the beauty of their dreams."
—Eleanor Roosevelt

Life is a numbers game—luck has very little to do with it. Even Warren Buffet does not have a 100 percent success rate. One might think that the ticklish nature of sports plays well into the hands of the lucky, and that money-making endeavors can be more predictable.

But this is simply not true. Risk is part of every win. In Chapter Seven I quoted the great golfer Ben Hogan, who described his sport as, "a game of misses."

The ball is stationary, and until it leaves terra firma all factors are known, tried, and practiced infinitum. Yet, even the best golfer cannot predict how their swing will go.

So to win, they swing at all of them like this will be the hole in one.

The winner knows that he cannot know how it will go. And the rest of humanity thinks you can. So they wait before putting their full effort behind something, they wait for certainty that they will win.

And they are still waiting!

This kind of thinking won't make you a Babe Ruth. And what is more, you'll also end up with something much worse: Low expectations.

We need dreams in order to thrive, and all dreams must be unrealistic.

This is the definition of a dream: Based on what you know, and what is possible, then it is not possible to do what you want. That is a dream.

When President Kennedy committed America to go to the moon he readily admitted the technology did not exist to get us there.

He specifically said we need a goal greater than that which our skills, talents, and knowledge permit.

Why?

Because that is the way to improve all of those things.

And the only way to do that is to take what we know to their limit, and then put one step forward.

Obviously, this is a recipe for failure.

But it's what has to happen to put a man on the moon.

This is a picture many of us were raised with:

© Ivelin Radkov, courtesy of Shutterstock.com

But, this is the reality:

© Ivelin Radkov, courtesy of Shutterstock.com

Failure is not failure. Failure is not the end. Winners know that within every failure are the seeds to success.

"Giving up is the final solution to a temporary problem."
—Anonymous Holocaust survivor

Orville and Wilbur Wright didn't understand aerodynamics enough to succeed when they dreamed of creating a flying machine, but in the process of trying, and mostly in the process of failure, they learned what was necessary to make a heavier than air machine soar.

I am absolutely certain this book will change the world. I know this because I learned what I did wrong from my previous book.

What is more, I can tell you in all honesty that I thought that book would change the world too. And I can also tell you, that was not the first book that I was convinced would change the world.

This thinking will eventually and inevitably create a book that will change the world.

As long as I don't lower my expectations.

If not for this goal of changing the world, I could not be bothered to write.

"We're here to put a dent in the universe. Otherwise why else even be here?"
—Steve Jobs

It's not motivation that creates success. It's knowing you are going to succeed that creates motivation.

A general who can convince his or her soldiers that success

is inevitable will find a very motivated army. Trying to create self-motivation without believing the future is bright is like trying to fly a kite indoors. Motivation is the wind in your sails.

The more you believe your next swing is going to go down in history, then the more certain you can be . . . it will!

And the more you believe tomorrow is going to be incredible, the more youthful you will be today.

Youth is not defined by the total of all your heartbeats, or some abstract number on a calendar. Youth is a factor of how great you think tomorrow is going to be.

As we said before, the higher your number for tomorrow, the younger you are today. It's not up to the mirror to decide how old you are. It's up to you. Make tomorrow's number higher, and despite the number on your birth certificate you will be able to slow the aging down—even turn it backward.

It's not winning that makes you youthful, it's being youthful that makes you win.

> ## "Make our days alive again, just as they used to be."
> ### —Lamentations 5:21

CHAPTER 22
IF
(Bringing it all together)

"Luck, good and bad, happens to everyone, whether we like it or not."

Imagine a giant vacuum cleaner so powerful that when pointed in the right direction it could suck the dust right off the moon.

That's what "if thinking" will do to your motivation.

Say these words and you can give up right now: "If only I had their luck."

You will never find a winner ascribing their success to luck.

This is not arrogance; it's simply an awareness of reality.

That doesn't mean they weren't lucky, and it doesn't mean they aren't fully cognizant of their luck. I have spoken to many a successful person, and without a doubt, they all know how lucky they have been.

This is not a contradiction.

That is because luck won't make anyone a winner—it's what you do with luck that makes you win.

Jim Collins and Morten Hansen

Jim Collins and Morten Hansen, in their book *Great by*

Choice, Uncertainty, Chaos, and Luck—Why Some Thrive Despite Them All, point out that successful people use good luck to their advantage and mitigate the bad, and everyone else does the opposite.

Viewing success as the product of luck forces you, by default, to believe you are not lucky.

When Dave Brailsford took over Britain's professional cycling team he faced one very stubborn fact: In the Tour de France's hundred-plus-year history, no Englishman had ever won.

It would be easy for him to think past performance was a good indication of future success, or lack thereof. I would not be surprised if more than a few British cyclists had concluded they (the English) aren't very lucky.

But this is the problem with luck, as soon as you view someone else as lucky, you immediately consider yourself not lucky. This thinking creates a self-fulfilling failure. People who view themselves as unlucky don't try, because there is no point.

This is something for you to ponder: How much of your life do you view as a product of luck, or the lack thereof?

This is the amazing thing. Within three years of taking the job, Brailsford's team won the Tour and did so again, four more times.

What was the explanation? Brailsford made it a point to find all the weaknesses in the team, and then sought out every method of improvement.

"The whole principle," Brailsford explains, "came from the idea that if you broke down everything you could think of that goes into riding a bike, and then improved it by 1 percent, you would get a significant increase when you put them all together."

And if you think you can replicate his success by doing what he did, you would have completely missed the point of this book.

Let me explain.

Imagine getting a ten-page questionnaire from your boss covering issues from personal hygiene to what kind of gas you put in your car. At the next company-wide meeting the CEO explains the importance of the questions by telling the story of Dave Brailsford, and tells his staff that if they, too, improve everything by 1 percent the company would become the leader in their field.

And he means everything. He emphasizes that Brailsford improved the obvious, like the bicycle seats, but also the not so obvious, such as changing the hand soap.

I would not be surprised if many of the employees would think such suggestions ridiculous. Some employees would refuse to participate, and more would just fudge the answers. Still others might start looking for other employment.

You can't do what winners do. You have to think like they think.

Brailsford could never have accomplished that level of improvement without changing his team's thinking.

"Until you get the inside of you right, your outer is never going to be right."
—Dabo Swinney

And he could never have convinced his team to do what needed to be done unless they all bought into the dream.

The key is future thinking. The more excited you are about the future, the more everything else works.

Once they bought into the vision of the future, then present thinking came naturally. It's easy for people to improve just 1 percent if the goal is big enough—and Brailsford made it enough.

"Solving big problems is easier than solving little problems."
—Sergey Brin, co-founder of Google

Present thinking is about change and fun: What do we need to change, and how do we have fun doing it?

Once Brailsford's team bought into the idea that they really could win the Tour, they readily accepted the fact that they needed better pillows. When a cyclist is on tour, using the right pillow at night makes a huge difference in feeling refreshed.

Without future buy-in though, very few people are going to put up with any significant (or even insignificant) increase in discomfort.

As was mentioned in Chapter Five, there probably was no greater productivity in America than during the Second World War. No promised bonuses or any incentives were needed other than a gigantic goal, what Jim Collins calls the BHAG—Big Hairy Audacious Goal.

Change and creating greater efficiencies are not an obstacles. The only obstacle is in not imagining a great enough future. The greater the goal, the bigger the future, the more change people are willing to make in the present.

The only obstacle to great future thinking is cynicism, and the bigger the goal, the greater the chance of cynicism. I am sure many people told Brailsford to be realistic, and reminded him that the British are not lucky cyclists.

But let's ponder that for a moment. And while we are doing it, plug in your own life here too and maybe some dreams you actually have.

Picture in your head two English bicycle teams, Brailsford's and the previous one.

That previous one failed. But in the next two years Brailsford failed too.

Even though he and his team followed the 1 percent plan, they still failed. They believed in winning and put up a great fight, but nevertheless they didn't win until year three.

Up until the day that Brailsford's team finally won, both English teams would be disappointed. But until that day, which one of the two teams were having the most fun?

Which one learned the most about life?

Which one regrets trying in the first place?

And which one would do it all again?

Hands down, without a question, Brailsford and his team were having a ball.

Tough? Yes! Grueling? Yes! But fun? Absolutely.

And they would do it all again, even with failure!

When you shoot for something really big, your quality of life becomes just as big. Even if you lose!

"Tis better to have loved and lost Than never to have loved at all."
—Alfred Lord Tennyson

I've met some great people in my time, and some of the best were the resistance fighters of World War II. These people faced an impossible foe, outnumbered and outgunned by huge percentages. By all accounts, their military effectiveness was meager at best, their victories small and generally inconsequential. But I never met a resistance fighter who regretted a minute of it.

Why don't we all aim for things like that? Why don't we take our goals for the year and triple them?

Because we would rather avoid disappointment than experience the fun.

The reason your life is not more exciting right now has nothing to do with your current circumstances—it has to do with your future. The closer your future is to the sun, the more thrilling and exciting it will be.

Once Brailsford fought off the doubters, even those on his own team, everything else came naturally.

As soon as you find your future dream, the next step will be obvious. It's keeping away those who doubt you that is tough, and that sometimes includes your own self-doubt.

For any previous British team, finding their own weaknesses would have been embarrassing. Similarly, for any business it's embarrassing. It's embarrassing because you don't have a goal big enough.

If a CEO can't discuss weaknesses with the team, it's because they don't have a vision exciting enough to make the employees want to find those weaknesses and change them.

Once you get future thinking, then the other two types of thinking (present and past) fit together exquisitely like a jigsaw puzzle.

Brailsford didn't win immediately; it took a while. But disappointment at the losses along the way didn't create low expectations. The past was a place to learn from so they could improve, not a source for lowering goals and expectations.

It's all about creating that "Going to Disneyland" anticipation of a six-year-old. Winners do this. Brailsford did this. Orville did this. Buffet did this.

You can do this too.

When my son was just a little tyke I bought him a toy car. But from his reaction, you might have thought I had bought him a sixty-foot yacht. He was jumping up and down, and if his skin wasn't sewn on tight I am sure he would have left it behind running to get the present.

A teenager getting their first car is similarly living a really big thrill.

However, a fifty-year-old waiting for their first Bentley to arrive will not be staying up till the wee hours looking through the window for the delivery like the seventeen-year-old waiting for grandma's twenty-year-old jalopy.

That doesn't mean fifty-year-olds have nothing to look forward to, it's just that they need a different and higher category of thrill.

A six-year-old will be thrilled with a toy truck, Disneyland, or even an ice cream. But a fifty-year-old is not going to be thrilled with a car (no matter how many buttons it has) like the one I bought for my son for less than ten dollars.

It's easy to see now why people get lost. They want the thrill, but feel they are just too old for cars, houses, and even jobs. Yes, they can have a thrill, but they can't have it from the past. They have to upgrade.

It was because they were in their thirties that Orville and Wilbur had to imagine something really big to get their thrill.

"We could hardly wait to get up in the morning."
—Wilbur Wright

Finding your goal is the key, one that is so thrilling you can "hardly wait to get up in the morning." And even though it might not pop out for you now, the more you read (and re-read) this book, the closer you will get. The desire to find your "Disneyland goal," in and of itself, is already future thinking, and will start to bring the other parts of your puzzle together.

Start now, and within a very short time you will see progress.

It's time to erase the bullseye you have painted around the spot where you are standing. Now is the time shoot for the exciting places you really want to get to in life.

CHAPTER 23

Don't Give Up

"If you seek it like silver, and search for it like treasure..."
—King Solomon, Proverbs, 2:4-5

What is the difference between silver and treasure?
Imagine inheriting an enormous island, totaling thousands of square miles, but far from any civilization. Using satellites you determine that somewhere on this island is a massive deposit of silver worth billions. Unfortunately, the technology can't tell you where on the island it is located.

What do you do?

Gather as many people as you can, give them all a shovel and plot out a path to dig. And keep digging.

Just make sure that you remember where you dug, so you don't go over the same place twice.

In other words, learn from your mistakes. Learn from what didn't work.

That's what learning from a mistake is. You dug here, it wasn't there, don't do it again. Finished. No guilt or blame, just a lesson.

Now a slightly different scenario: Same island, but this time it's not silver but buried treasure. Again worth billions.

What do you do this time?

You would not systematically dig like you did for silver; this hunt will require thought.

If you were burying treasure, where would you put it?

Someone burying treasure isn't going to put it in a place that another will accidentally find. Nor will they put it in a place that anyone would think of; it's the same reason it is best to have an ATM pin number that no one else would consider. (There are 10,000 different possible four-digit ATM PIN numbers, but almost 11 percent of PINs are 1234. Source: *Huffington Post*)

King Solomon, the wisest of all, told us three thousand years ago that in order to win you need the determination to find silver and the ingeniousness to find treasure.

Silver

Why do people give up? Because they don't realize there is a very finite number of failures. It's not an infinite number—each time you try, you get closer to success.

"Many of life's failures are people who did not realize how close they were to success when they gave up."
—Thomas A. Edison

The only way to lose is to not learn from your mistakes. Just as in the search for silver, if you keep digging in the same spot you are never going to find it. There will be an infinite number of tries if you don't learn from your mistakes.

Winners know it's a numbers game, and eventually they

will win, because when you are willing to learn from your mistakes there will be a limited number of losses.

"I have not failed. I've just found 10,000 ways that won't work." —Thomas A. Edison

This is how a winner thinks.

Edison knew that there were a finite number of times that he would fail. And as long as he didn't give up, as long as he learned from his mistakes, then eventually and inevitably, he would find the solution and win. And that's true for you too.

Each of your failures will eliminate one of those wrong possibilities.

The prize is still out there, and as long as you don't dig in the same location, you will eventually find it.

It's not a failure; it's one step closer to success.

You have tried many things, and have failed at many too. But great success is ahead of you.

Cross off another number toward your 10,000th try.

Treasure

We all have had goals. And we all have been frustrated when they didn't go the way we thought they should. That's because our thinking is the same as everyone else's.

And treasure is never buried where people think it should be.

Every goal is a treasure—and it's always buried in a place no one would think of. It's buried somewhere else.

"This 'telephone' has too many shortcomings to be seriously considered as a means of communication. The device is inherently of no value to us."
—Western Union internal memo, 1876

Don't think the folks at Western Union were fools, or any more foolish than the rest of us. The great success we are all seeking is hidden like treasure. In hindsight, yes, it's easy to see. But what King Solomon is telling us, treasure/success is not where everyone thinks it should be.

That's why great success is so startling. It's easy to criticize IBM for missing the PC boom, Kodak for not getting into digital, and countless other stories of missed opportunities. But while it's really difficult to see them, nevertheless, they are real and significant. They are right in front of you. You just need to uncover them.

When you have exhausted everything you know, that's when you discover the unexpected.

Unfortunately, that moment is also the moment many people give up.

Don't!

EPILOGUE

LOSERS

You might have noticed that I have awkwardly avoided the term "loser" throughout this book. Phrases such as "People who don't win" could be more easily stated as "Losers."

The reason I've avoided the word is because there is no such thing as a loser.

The world is not conveniently divided between winners and so-called losers. It's divided between winners and people who are not winners. Yet.

Yes, you have failed at many things—as has the rest of humanity. That is something we all have in common. But nothing precludes you, or anyone, from using any and all of those failings as the source for great and stunning success.

And the way that you use them, is by learning from them.

In this context, the word failure is also inappropriate. It's only a failure if you give up.

"A man can fail many times,
but he isn't a failure
until he begins to blame somebody else."
—John Burroughs

My dear reader, you have invested a lot of time and energy in searching for your silver mine.

That is a lot of experience.

That experience is priceless, because within that experience are the lessons you need to find your treasure.

Now please, read this book again, and it will bring you to WIN.

Acknowledgments

Nothing you have read is from me. It all comes from our *Instructions for Living*, otherwise known as the *Torah*, and often referred to as the *Bible*.

The *Mesilit Yesharim* by Rav Moshe Chaim Luzato Ztl, is also threaded throughout *WIN*.

Both are wisdom not of this world.

I had phenomenal teachers who helped me along this path. Foremost was Rav Noah Weinberg Ztl. Also, Rabbi Sammy Kassin and Rabbi Tom Meyer.

I also had amazing parents who taught me to believe in the future. I owe it all to them!

Of course, none of this would be possible without my amazing and incredible, love of my life, wife, who lives all that I have written.

Plus, three people I cannot thank enough. Verne Harnish, at the next election everyone should write in his name for president. Paul Akers took a piece of coal and turned it into a diamond. Jonah Bornstein, the publisher and editor. Jonah put his life and soul into this and despite many challenges along the way, never gave up. There is a piece of Jonah in this book.

And a big thank you to all the people who made this book a possibility:

Sara Abergel

Tammy and Gene Berman

Amanda and Aharon Boltax

Joe Bormel

Rabbi Josh Boretsky

Ilka V. Chavez

Barry and Yvonne Cohen

Albert and Karen Costilo

Paul and Gail Chod

David and Renee Dalva

Aaron and Linda Dayan

Albert and Claire Dwoski

Mark and Nava Ely
Vlad and Sophia Fastovsky
Barry Friedberg
Carla and Neal Freed
Javier and Ana Goldin
Rich and Kate Goldman
Lisa and Robert Gray
Jeff Green
Mark and Keri Green
Dr. Neil Green
Richard and Miriam Greene
Brooke Greenwald
   and Jamey Charapp
Daniel and Pamela Ely
Debbie and Jerry Greenspan
Nancee Gross
Ira and Miriam Grossman
Jay Heltzer
Karl and Rocio Hiller
Marc and Gail Isaacson
Kahlil Jackson
Finiana Joseph
Liz and Amir Kaplan
Dr. David and Rachel Katz
Edward & Cynthia Katz
Shmuel and Chava Kott
Rabbi Eliezer Kreiser
Mitch and Karen Kuflick
Avi and Ayelet Lichtash
Dr. David Lieberman

Erik and Connie Lindenauer
Steven Loewy
Shelley Blumberg-Lorenzana
Louis and Manette Mayberg
Ronald and Marcelle Mervis
Shraga Murik
Daniel and Tova Mosesson
Wendy and Oren Penn
Daniel and Ilana Ratner
Hector and Delores Rivas
Angela Romero
Ted Rose
Rabbi and Mrs. Saffer
Gil and Bonnie Schwardron
Sandy Sherman
Yakov ben Solomon
Elisha and Anabel Stein
Sen. Richard Stone
Stanley Tate
Mark and Judy Teitelbaum
Rabbi Mordechai Tussie
Todd Walderman
Rav Simcha Weinberg
Robyn Weiner
Dr. Yechiel and Zita Weinstein
Josh Whisler
Rabbi Menachem Winter
Samuel Williamowsky
Richard and Cindy Zitelman
Nelly and Boris Zusin

In memory of Sheldon Spector, M.D.,
whose life was about giving

AND THANK YOU, FOR WITHOUT YOU
THERE WOULD BE NO POINT